Praise for *Unwavering*

"You might be all powerful, confident, and perfect but there is a little Nellie in you. There is certainly a little Nellie in me. We better start doing some things that are uncomfortable because our planet, people, and our businesses need strong leaders. Nellie changed lives and a great organization by being courageous. She proves repeatedly that the people around you change when you do. Great companies have an uncommon proportion of leaders like Nellie, and I have the data to prove it."

—Michael C. Bush,
CEO of Great Place To Work and global authority on high-trust, high-performance workplace cultures

"In Unwavering, *Nellie Borrero shares how she has led the charge for diversity and inclusion to ensure that everyone belongs. In her authentic voice, she brings to light the urgency for change today and inspires readers to take action. If you read just one book about the power of belonging and how you can be a champion for a culture of inclusion in your organization, read* Unwavering.*"*

—Jacqui Canney,
Chief People Officer, ServiceNow

*"*Unwavering *will change the way leaders think, feel, and behave—no matter who you are, or where you are in your career. The book offers unexpected candor, timely insights, and battle-tested solutions. Rarely do you find so many resources in one place."*

—Douglas R. Conant,
former Fortune 500 CEO, champion of 21st-century leadership, and *New York Times* bestselling author

"*Iconic leadership is inclusive leadership. No one knows that better than Nellie Borrero. Her personal story of over 30 years at a top global company is truly "unwavering"—where she faced the same kinds of hurdles, challenges, and opportunities that so many people still deal with at work today. No matter what your background, position, or company, Nellie's book will mandate that you do more, because (as the data show) growth leadership is inclusive leadership.*"

—Rachel Cooke,
Chief Operating Officer, Brandon Hall Group

"*Powerful and honest! Nellie Borrero's story of her courageous rise from the Bronx to Director at Accenture will keep you laughing, cringing at the missteps, and inspired until the very end. Filled with the raw truth of what it is to be a woman of color in leadership, Nellie's story is about remarkable challenges, passion, and determination to make this company's inclusion a competitive advantage. She shares her award-winning strategies, starting with smart moves everyone can make on Monday morning to think bigger.* Unwavering *is a must read for executives, HR, and people everywhere looking to make their organizations better because we can't wait any longer to get talent right.*"

—Dr. Marshall Goldsmith,
Thinkers50 #1 Executive Coach and *New York Times* bestselling author, including *The Earned Life*

"*Deeply personal, with vivid stories that evoke strong emotions in the reader, Borrero's book brings to the surface the challenges that so many of us face in the workplace and provides a roadmap for how to overcome them.*"

—Dr. Stefanie K. Johnson,
Thinkers50 guru, professor at CU Boulder's Leeds School of Business, and author of the *Wall St. Journal* bestseller *Inclusify*

"Unwavering *is the book that gives the inspiration to dismantle bias that leads to lifelong transformation, and celebration of inclusivity of all. Nellie's reflections are remnants of the past that bring light to the urgency of today. While her experiences may shock some, they will empower all to be change agents and inspire others to stand as allies. Do yourself a favor, if you really are seeking to understand the power and impact of belonging, get this book today and another for a colleague or mentee."*

—Leah McGowen-Hare, MSEd,
Senior Vice President, Salesforce

"A book full of lived truths, Nellie Borrero's Unwavering *starts with personal, powerful, deeply resonant stories. For those who wish to unleash their under-recognized greatness—whether you are an "awkward ally" who can do more to help others find their greatness, or you come from a diverse community and have faced some of Nellie's same barriers—this book gives you a sense of agency to win together."*

—Sanyin Siang,
Director of Duke University's Coach K Leadership and
Ethics Center, Thinkers50 guru, and CEO advisor

"Nellie Borrero is a one-of-a-kind human being who has focused her career on uplifting others through the power of inclusion. Accenture has evolved into a globally recognized diverse and best place to work in large part due to Nellie's grit and humanity. She's taken her 30-year career at Accenture and openly shared it as a continued effort to create change. Get the full story, and how you can become a champion for inclusion in your company, in Unwavering."

—Rosa Ramos-Kwok,
JPMorgan Chase Managing Director and
Board Chair of the Hispanic IT Executive Council

"This book is important for everyone to read, process, and absorb. Her premise is truly about a successful business in the 21st century. I have always thought of diversity and inclusion as "basic business." If you don't have a broad set of talent, don't understand your broad base of customers, and don't understand the broad base of suppliers your company depends upon, your business will not achieve the performance levels of those that do. Talent has proven to be an engine of growth and innovation—all kinds of talent, including diverse backgrounds, ethnicities, and experiences. Companies, organizations, and governments with a truly diverse mix of talent have been shown to outperform those with limited or no diversity. Nellie's book, Unwavering, brings that into clear focus. In her career, Nellie has exemplified an action-oriented pioneer and leader as she has ascended to Managing Director of Global Inclusion & Diversity at Accenture. Nellie represents the heart and soul of Accenture. She lives it and breathes it. Her book serves as a manual for how to value all people, and how to bring together diverse talents to build a competitive advantage and a world-class culture."

—Sol Trujillo,
Founder and Chairman, Trujillo Group,
Chairman of the Latino Donor Collaborative, and
Co-Founder of L'ATTITUDE

UNWAVERING

Foreword by **JULIE SWEET**

NELLIE BORRERO

UNWAVERING

REJECTING BIAS, IGNITING CHANGE, CELEBRATING INCLUSION

WILEY

Published by John Wiley & Sons, Inc., Hoboken, New Jersey.
Published simultaneously in Canada.

For general information on our other products and services or for technical support, please contact our Customer Care Department within the United States at (800) 762-2974, outside the United States at (317) 572-3993 or fax (317) 572-4002.

Wiley also publishes its books in a variety of electronic formats. Some content that appears in print may not be available in electronic formats. For more information about Wiley products, visit our web site at www.wiley.com.

Library of Congress Cataloging-in-Publication Data is Available:

ISBN: 9781394239870 (cloth)
ISBN: 9781394239887 (ePub)
ISBN: 9781394239894 (ePDF)

Cover Design: Wiley
Cover Image: © epic/Adobe Stock
Author Photo: © Brett Deutsch, Deutsch Photography

SKY10064711_011224

I dedicate this book to:

*My parents, Jose and Georgina, who set a foundation full of love,
instilling an inner sense of spirituality, self-empowerment, and pride*

*My husband, Ken, who has lovingly and unselfishly cheered me on
throughout all phases of our journey together*

*My children, Ginaly and Kenny, whose daily love nourishes me,
infusing me with incredible joy and purpose*

*My grandson, Liam, who has reminded me how amazing life is
through a child's love and imagination*

Contents

Foreword

The success of Accenture is completely entwined with our focus on diversity, equity, and inclusion. With a culture and sense of belonging, we have better financial performance, attract the best talent, and live our core values. But it was not always this way at our company.

In 2010, when I joined Accenture, then-CEO Pierre Nanterme said to me, "We aren't leaders. We are fast followers." And we both knew that posture was not sufficient to ensure our success. Just a few years later, we set the ambition to be innovation-led and to rotate our company from being less than 20% digital, cloud and security to 70% by 2020. We recognized that you cannot lead in innovation—and reinvent the core of your business—by being a fast follower. And you cannot be an innovator without a wide range of perspectives, expertise, and insight. That was the point where diversity became a business priority.

The business rationale is clear: talent is a competitive differentiator. To be successful in the coming decade, companies will need to access, create, and unlock the potential of talent. And if leaders do not attract diverse talent, they shrink their pool of talent by default—leading to less of a competitive advantage.

So we set the strategy and the goals, collected data, and began to hold our leaders accountable, just as we do with our financial priorities. And in 2015, as CEO of Accenture North America, I published externally—for the first time in our industry—our US workforce demographic data for gender, race and ethnicity, persons with disabilities, and veterans. We did so with a clear vision in mind: transparency builds trust. Our numbers were not good at the outset, so we doubled down. And we began to attract more diverse talent, not because we were where we wanted to be, but because people knew we were committed to fostering a culture where everyone can be themselves and reach their potential both personally and professionally.

None of this would have happened without Nellie Borrero.

Nellie's journey is Accenture's journey. In her words, she has led the way in "rejecting biases, taking the space, and owning it with good intention." She has helped Accenture—and countless companies and individuals—move from aspiration to action. Her determination and relentless focus on doing the right thing for everyone in the room, even when it is incredibly difficult, have moved the needle from a lack of understanding (and sometimes even blind resistance to change) to a welcome and necessary reality of diversity through intention, inclusion through choice, and equality through everyday actions.

I greatly value my relationship with Nellie—and I am inspired by her journey. She has been instrumental in helping me become the leader I aspire to be, through her fearless feedback and clear counsel.

For decades, Nellie has traveled the world, sharing lessons learned with underrepresented communities and coaching generations of leaders on how best to lead others, particularly around diversity. In these pages, she offers practical advice on negotiating cultural collisions, creating your own brand of courage, cultivating a sense of belonging, and knowing your worth. At the heart of all this is Nellie's personal story—the ups and downs, with nothing held back. This is a book about human potential and possibility, grounded in real emotion and her boundless empathy.

It is not always easy reading, because it is not intended to be. Diversity and inclusion are challenging issues. Nellie raises the tough questions about belonging, marginalizing, and self-minimalizing that we must ask about the people we work with, and ourselves, especially if we are leaders. What does it feel like to be uncomfortable in your own skin—to feel marginalized and alone? To have your abilities questioned by others? And to question them yourself?

Through her honesty, her openness, and her practical guidance, Nellie is igniting the change she wants to see in the world. Guided by her insightful and hopeful book, we can work together toward a future where everyone is seen, heard, and valued—and everyone celebrates inclusion.

Julie Sweet
Chair and Chief Executive Officer, Accenture

UNWAVERING

Introduction: The Power of One Question

Several years ago, my colleague Carolina and I were debating a career opportunity that would have evolved the work that I'd been doing to have a more global reach. It was an expanded role that would have undoubtedly propelled my career to new leadership heights and the type of professional advancement that I had visualized for quite some time. Yet instead of being fully excited, I sat there listing all of the reasons—or more accurately, all of the excuses—why it was not a sound strategic move for me at that time. I felt a heaviness that robbed me of my freedom to get excited and feel truly joyous about the opportunity.

As I relentlessly added to the list of negatives, Carolina asked me in a very direct and deliberate manner, "Nellie, who in your past has made you believe that you are not good enough?" Her stare was piercing and somewhat intimidating. Although I knew in my heart that her question came from a genuinely good place—she was a team member who reported to me and we'd known each other for quite some time at that point—my mind immediately went to, "What did she just have the audacity to ask me? Seriously, why would she ask me that?"

I paused for a moment, hoping that my body language adequately concealed my defensiveness. With conviction and a serious attitude, I replied, "Absolutely no one." I was not willing to be exposed, and I wanted my reply to end the conversation. I redirected the conversation towards other topics we needed to address. But as decisive as my answer was, I couldn't deny the unpleasant sting that resonated inside of me. It was obvious that she had touched a nerve.

At home that evening, I still could not shake off the discomfort of Carolina's question. I tried to shift my attention to my normal evening routine. I turned on the news for some distracting noise and tore through the kitchen, flinging open the refrigerator and cupboards to quickly cook dinner, but none of it helped. With every dash of seasoning I shook into the pot, I could, in almost perfect synchronization, hear myself repeat each word from that provocative question: *"Who. Made. You. Believe. You're. Not. Good. Enough?"*

I knew it was time to stir one of the pots on the stove, but I was too distracted to do so. One by one, faster and faster, memories from my childhood flooded my mind. Those moments, experiences, and incidents that had impacted me deeply and shaped my beliefs vividly reappeared, accompanied by a swirl of emotions. The questions of self-reflection came in quick succession. Had I subconsciously been showing up as if I were not good enough? If so, had this belief inadvertently affected or slowed down my career progression or personal brand? What opportunities have I missed along the way as a result? Have I been too passive or too complacent because I subconsciously don't believe myself to be good enough? I was feeling anxious, and angry, but also curious. I knew that no matter how uncomfortable, I needed to dig deeper and find the answers.

My Early Days

I learned very early in life how to make myself virtually invisible to those who did not look like me. Standing in the elevator of an apartment complex that my parents worked hard to get us into, my mother's orders rang loudly in my young ears: "Be still. Be silent. No talking, laughing, or acting silly. No eye contact with anyone." My sister and I did exactly as we were told whenever we entered the lobby of our building. In the elevator, I almost felt like I was holding my breath as I watched the floor numbers ascend. By the time we finally reached the 23rd floor, I could barely wait to get into our apartment, where the outside world no longer mattered, and we were free to be our authentic Nuyorican selves.

It was the mid-'70s, and my parents had managed somehow to secure a North Bronx apartment in a massive complex with very few minority families at the time. My parents felt incredibly fortunate to raise their daughters in such a good and safe neighborhood, but they also had no delusions about the real world. My mother's lobby rules weren't given out of meanness or malice. They were intended to protect our innocence from conceivable prejudices, from people we assumed would not embrace minorities, while also teaching us not to feed into others' biases and perceptions about minority children.

My parents were both raised in a small town in Puerto Rico called Juncos, but they did not meet one another until they were young adults living in New York City, trying to navigate a better life. Both were bright and smart, but each had limited resources. My dad was recruited from Puerto Rico at the age of 17 to pick tomatoes at a farm in New Jersey. My mother left Puerto Rico right after high school due to the lack of opportunities at the time and began her working career as a seamstress in a factory. My father went on to enroll in the military, where he served in the army. I was born in Manhattan, and we lived in the city until I completed first grade, which is when my parents decided to go back to Puerto Rico.

My strong sense of fairness began to emerge during those early years and continued to develop throughout my life. I didn't know a word of Spanish when we moved to Puerto Rico because we were raised speaking English in New York. I was supposed to be in the second grade, but because I didn't know Spanish, they held back my progress by placing me half day in the first-grade class and half day in the second-grade class. From that very young age, I found myself in an environment where I did not feel smart. One day the teacher asked me in Spanish to look at a page in the math book. I didn't understand her instructions, so she hit my hand with a ruler. It was all very confusing for me. Eventually, school did get better, and I learned Spanish. But when I was in sixth grade, my parents suddenly decided to move us back to New York, and of course I had forgotten all of my English by that time.

Upon moving back, I had to go to a junior high school in the Bronx, which was very different and challenging for me. I was a skinny little girl with long, wavy, thin hair and big glasses. As with most girls that age, I grappled with my self-confidence. There were days that I thought I was the cutest thing on earth and other days when I struggled to find even one good quality about the girl in the mirror. Because I didn't know any English upon returning to New York, they placed me in a special education class instead of an English as a Second Language (ESL) class. I was in a classroom with kids who had behavioral issues and I felt intimidated every day. I couldn't understand what others were saying, so I would just sit there and mimic what the other students were doing. I saw kids drawing on a desk, so I drew on a desk, too. But I'd be the one who got sent to the principal's office. The principal's secretary, a white woman who understood a little bit of Spanish and would speak with me while waiting for the principal, was the only one who realized that I was in the wrong class. She told the administrators that I did not belong in special education, and they moved me into a mainstream class.

Things remained challenging, though. One day, I got up the courage to raise my hand and try to say something. The teacher said to the class, "Can someone explain to Nellie how we speak in this country?" It was so humiliating at the time, but it infuriates me now. She said "this country" as if Puerto Rico isn't a commonwealth of the US. As if I'm not an American citizen. If I had been fluent in English, I probably would have given that teacher a much-needed lesson about US territories.

I became aware of bias and prejudice outside of school as well. At the time, my father worked at the US Postal Service. It was a huge deal for him. Getting a government job with a pension was a significant step towards financial security. There weren't many minorities working at the postal service in the late '60s and early '70s. There was a lot of racial tension and my father experienced racism firsthand. Being called derogatory names like "spic" was commonplace. But my father learned to tolerate the ignorance because he understood the bigger goal of providing for his family. He learned to lay low, not draw attention to himself, and simply do his job. I often wonder how much he was forced to endure and what inner struggles he dealt with while doing so. My dad was larger than life in my eyes, an avid reader, and the smartest person I knew.

My mom had her own strengths as well. Her skills as a seamstress were unparalleled. She would design patterns and sew beautiful clothes for my sister and me. She had endless potential, but her reality was limited to factories in the garment district of New York City, where the working conditions were far from desirable. Once, while I was in college, I tried to surprise her at work. I had never been to her job before, but I was going to be in the area, so I decided to go see her at the factory on 14th Street. As the doors opened to my mother's floor, I was saddened by the number of people crowded together working with almost no personal space. Huge fans blew dust from the fabrics around in the air. I saw my mom and told the man at the door that I was there to see her. In a very intimidating manner, he demanded to know why. I was so thrown off by his aggression that I just left without speaking to my mom.

At home, the nurturing was always on overdrive, and my parents created an environment abundant with love. I always felt safe and protected in our home. My mother worked during the day and my dad worked at night, so there was always a parent in the house watching over us. We were raised with discipline, religion, home cooking, chores, games, and cultural awareness. Latin music played every Sunday afternoon and serenaded us into the night. I learned to dance salsa standing on my dad's feet while he danced around our living room, spinning me around to the rhythm of those soul-captivating beats. Those days taught me to love salsa and I have danced it throughout my life. It's become a "happy place" that I still turn to when I need to feel centered and grounded.

Recognizing the Limits to Reaching My Full Potential

Although I reminisce about my childhood with fondness, I also recognize the insularity of my upbringing. It disadvantages a child not to have experiences outside of their neighborhood. For a while, my entire world encompassed a few blocks. That type of limitation can keep a child from reaching their full potential. It's a loss that you don't even recognize when growing up; at least my sister and I didn't. How can you know that there is a world full of incredible opportunities when you've never been exposed to the broader possibilities?

As a teenager living in the Bronx, I created a narrative for myself that excluded the things that I never expected to attain. I kept a mental list of possessions and experiences that were not meant for people like me. We didn't grow up with a lot of disposable income. We couldn't afford a new car, so my dad had an old used car he treasured. It had a gaping hole in the floor of the driver's side, which my dad covered with several pieces of cardboard. But we never felt sad, concerned, or even embarrassed by it. Instead, we laughed and called it our Flintstones car. My dad appreciated that old car so much that he protected it from thieves by hooking a thick chain from the steering wheel to the brakes and placing a huge lock across the steering wheel. "Gotta make sure the car is still here tomorrow," he would say. My sister and I laughed at the thought of someone actually wanting to steal that car. But my father protected it as if it was the most expensive and luxurious car in the world. I learned

Two self-imposed questions rescued me from remaining captive in the "limited belief" cycle: Why not me? Why not for me?

to drive in that car, and looking back, I appreciate how my father took such great care of the things he was able to afford.

Because I didn't grow up having what seemed like luxuries, the thought of owning a home with a beautiful picket fence felt too far-fetched to me. Being able to wear diamond earrings or elegant pearls was beyond my imagination. I didn't allow myself to dream beyond my surroundings, and I sometimes wonder if I wanted to protect myself from the possible disappointments of dreaming big. Two self-imposed questions rescued me from remaining captive in the "limited belief" cycle: Why not me? Why not for me? I wanted answers that would point me towards more, help me break free of limitations, and encourage me to see possibilities through a broader and unfamiliar lens.

While my self-imposed unattainable list was extensive, I felt a pressing inner desire for more. I knew the inner sense of restlessness that I constantly felt was something I didn't have the ability or energy to ignore. I felt that I was different, and the expectations placed on me by my family and friends felt high and grandiose. I desperately wanted to make my parents proud. I wanted to provide for them. I angrily began to reject the notion of settling for what my surroundings dictated. I wasn't willing to accept the TV images that showcased Latinas as maids or crime victims. I wanted to believe that I deserved more. But I also didn't relate to the images that showcased attractive white women as professionals or well-groomed, stay-at-home moms. It was all quite conflicting. The news was filled with troubling stories about minority communities, but I was determined to achieve something different.

My parents had hopeful but guarded expectations of the educational system. They wanted to believe that it would fairly

educate and guide their daughters, but they also understood the
reality for Latina girls in a public school with a high percentage
of minority students being taught by predominantly Caucasian
teachers. They had experienced the harsh realities of racism
firsthand, and my dad refused to let us be naïve about it. In a very
gentle but calculated way, he planted a seed about the racism
he believed we would experience. His words captured my
attention. "Teachers are not very interested or vested in your
learning. You are a minority," my dad would say in his typical
slow-paced, preachy tone, while looking over his glasses. "For
that reason, you need to try harder. Teaching kids like you is not
their priority." The message was not an angry one, just plainly
laid out as an effective way of teaching us that we had been
entrusted with a greater responsibility and burden simply because
of who we were or what we represented.

Each time I would hear him say it, I would ask myself, "Could
that really be true?" I wanted to reject such an awful reality. As a
teenager, I really wanted to believe that others, and particularly
my teachers, had an interest in my well-being. But the uneasiness
that my parents experienced about the education that my sister
and I would receive turned out to be accurate. The educators
that they entrusted with our young minds did the very minimum
when it came to shaping our futures. I had no clue how to
differentiate between Ivy League, private, state, or city colleges.
I had no understanding about the importance of the SATs. My
sole memory leading up to the SAT is that of my homeroom
teacher's daily reminders to show up with two No. 2 sharpened
pencils if we wanted to be admitted to the test. There were no
discussions about my interests or majors. In fact, the one meeting
that I did have with my senior year guidance counselor about my
interests turned out to be more damaging than useful.

I walked into his office and sat on the hard wooden chair across from him. I remember looking at his desk, intrigued by all of the different objects. From the paperwork and colored folders to the glass paperweight, the entire setting screamed of intelligence and success to me. I had such high expectations for our conversation. What would he recommend that I pursue? Teaching had been on my mind a lot. During my ninth-grade year, my father came home with a manual typewriter that he found in a trash bin. He cleaned it, adjusted the ribbon, and presented it to me. "Nellie, I want you to learn how to type," he said. "It will help you find a good job someday." I laid a blanket on the floor, placed that beautiful black typewriter on top of it, and began tapping away on those keys. I later took a typing class that I loved, and I still vividly remember the synchronized tap of typewriter keys as the teacher walked around calling out letters to practice. The way the teacher commanded that room had truly inspired me to become a teacher myself.

Sitting in my guidance counselor's office eager for guidance, I expected to hear the path to my future teaching career or another intriguing option. I had my notebook open and was ready to take notes. I gave him an inquisitive look and a shy smile of anticipation as he began to speak. "Nellie, after graduation, I recommend that you apply for a cashier in a department store." I almost gasped, and I immediately felt deflated. I wanted to be a teacher and my guidance counselor had just crushed that vision. I am still saddened by that memory. I vividly remember walking out of the room feeling completely devalued and confused. I wondered if he advised students who didn't look like me to go work in a department store instead of applying to college. Did he dash their hopes and dreams with one sentence? Probably not. Why didn't he see me as worthy of more? What right did he have to underestimate my life and abilities?

Thankfully, someone else saw fit to do the job that my guidance counselor failed to do that day. On my way home, I ran into an acquaintance named Linda who was a few years older than me. She mentioned that she had recently graduated from LaGuardia Community College with an associate's degree as a legal secretary and was loving her new job. She seemed so happy and accomplished, which was exactly what I wanted for my life. That conversation sparked something in me and gave me a plan: I would apply to LaGuardia Community College. This is where I chose a different path, one where my determination blossomed as I increasingly recognized my potential. I began to resist the societal limitations that, spoken or unspoken, had been clearly defined for me. My parents had surrounded me with love and a strong sense of self-worth. Though I didn't recognize it as a child, those loving deep roots had been directly combating the negativity I experienced outside of the home.

Attending LaGuardia turned out to be one of the best decisions of my life. My time there opened so many new opportunities. I was able to take advantage of their co-op program, which enabled students to attend school while working. I ended up getting a job at the NYU Graduate School Office of Career Services. As a result, I was able to pay my own tuition after only two quarters. My parents would have gladly paid for my tuition, but I was so happy to relieve them of that responsibility. I got up at 5:00 a.m. to take a bus and a train to work. I would then leave there at 5:00 p.m. and catch two trains to attend school at night. I took classes until 10:00 p.m. before catching two trains and a bus home. I would get there around 11:30 p.m. to find my mother waiting each night to serve me dinner. I'd then get up the next morning to do it all over again.

Working and going to school was a rigorous schedule, but completely worth it. The dean of the NYU Graduate School Office of Career Services saw such potential in me that he decided to offer me a full-time job as his assistant. My annual compensation was $12,500, which seemed like so much money to me at the time. He also encouraged me to apply to NYU upon graduating from LaGuardia. I did so successfully and attended NYU undergrad tuition-free due to my employment with the graduate school. After a while, I was offered a higher-paying job with a bank, and I decided that the increased compensation was best for me and my family. I resigned from my job with the graduate school and began employment with the bank. But what I didn't realize at the time was that the tuition reimbursement offered by the bank was not 100%, leaving me with a big tuition gap that I couldn't afford to pay. I didn't explore a student loan because I didn't know that was even an option. Not getting my bachelor's degree was not an option for me, though, so I ultimately opted to attend the more affordable Lehman College.

I did not attend either of my two college graduation ceremonies. For LaGuardia's, I felt that an associate degree was not worth celebrating. For Lehman College, I felt that my diploma was not NYU-caliber, so in my mind it was also not worth celebrating. In retrospect, I wish I had viewed both accomplishments differently. Those decisions created a lifelong pattern of not celebrating accomplishments and milestones throughout my life.

Answering the Uncomfortable Question

I find myself often asking, "Does this person really have an interest in my success?" That doubt has played into every professional relationship throughout my journey. It has made me question the authenticity of people in my professional life and impacted the process of building trust with them. Even though my parents undoubtedly always spoke with my best interests at heart, that childhood message created a wall that I still must break through in order to reach a place of comfort in a relationship.

Unfortunately, many young people still contend with a lack of assistance when seeking guidance about their futures. These seeds that we allow others to plant into our storyline can gain significant power within us. Their effects consistently creep in and out of our lives, impacting our choices. My eventual path in life would lead me along an incredible journey, defined by purpose and courage, but it also made me face some uncomfortable truths about myself, my insecurities, and those seeds that shaped me so many years ago.

Sometimes the very direct, hard-hitting, and gut-wrenching questions that we take exception to are exactly what we need to shake us up a bit. We all need those people along our journeys who will call us out, encourage us to step out of our comfort zone, and create a safe space for thoughtful and what would otherwise feel like difficult but liberating conversations. I was fortunate to have Carolina in my path at that pivotal moment and, in hindsight, I appreciate the self-reflection that her question sparked. For years, I had avoided having that candid conversation with myself, even though it was a conversation that needed to happen. I ultimately decided to embrace the expansion of my role eagerly, but not before taking a serious look at the source of my doubts. I realized that I was arguing myself out of an opportunity because it felt too risky and unfamiliar.

I had an opportunity to pave a new inroad for myself, but uncertainties had me at a bit of a disadvantage because I wasn't exactly clear what biases I would encounter within other cultures. I was accustomed to facing prejudices in the US, but I wasn't quite sure how that would show up in places like France, the UK, India, South Africa, and many other countries around the world, or if I had the courage to fight those biases. There was another internal conversation simultaneously underway, one that people of color will likely recognize. I was acknowledging the significance of being one of the few executives within the organization who represented my demographic, and I recognized the impact that my success or failure would have on the pipeline for others like me. This internal conversation was tied to the often unspoken but clearly understood phenomenon that, within the corporate environment, the actions of one person of an underrepresented group reflect on all within that group. That immense pressure feeds the doubts and hesitation that ultimately supersede what would otherwise be your aspirational, confident, and optimistic self.

But in spite of my fears, I faced all the uncertainties in the same way I had done throughout my entire career. I tapped into the best of my culture: our ability to understand the power of connections and how important relationships are in our professional and personal lives. In my cultural upbringing, we were expected to greet any visitor who came into our home. It did not matter what we were doing; it was mandatory that we stop to say hello and have a conversation. I always found that to be so annoying and disruptive, but it taught me a lot about how to interact with people, whether I'm comfortable with it or not. I see it with other members of minority communities as well. When people come into our spaces, we greet them as if we've known them forever. We immediately portray a welcoming warmth. Going into the expanded global opportunity, I focused on initially making connections with one or two people and nurturing relationships with them. Once that trust and rapport was established, those same people would become the ones to help me evolve that network. I was taught very early to appreciate the power of connections and that superpower helped me navigate those new challenges.

So, to answer the question that opened this book: Who in my past has made me believe that I am not good enough? Well, I have never felt that I am not good enough, but collective experiences have definitely had an impact in shaping the way I navigate my journey. I have faced the limited beliefs that can abruptly halt professionals of color and I directly challenged them.

The Complexities of Finding Belonging

Stay humble, and don't brag.

Let your hard work speak for itself.

Be grateful and patient.

Share your success by generously providing for others.

Respect elders and leaders—don't challenge them.

These lessons were drilled into my head from a young age by both my parents and my culture, and I've obediently adhered to them. On the surface, it all sounds very wise. But these mindsets can become obstacles when you are faced with the difficulty of navigating a corporate environment that often conflicts with the cultural norms that have been ingrained in you since childhood. Many people of color experience this type of collision. We grapple with the contradiction of staying humble while advocating for recognition and promotions. We struggle to suppress our discomfort with challenging leaders, colleagues, or peers, while reminding ourselves of the need to be grateful for the opportunity we currently have. We plunge into our work and exhaust our energy out of a need to prove ourselves beyond 100%, leaving us so depleted that we can't engage in the other important aspects (which we may or may not know about) of reaching our career goals. Instead, we resign ourselves to hoping or believing that our contributions are being valued.

Yet for those who are not familiar with our cultures, our approach to navigating the corporate environment is often misunderstood. For example, they may perceive our not speaking up in a meeting as disengaged, disinterested, not adding value, and not contributing. This can lead to lack of advocacy, support, and sponsorship, which can ultimately impact the trajectory of our careers. I became painfully aware of these challenges early on, when my cultural beliefs collided with the realisms of the fast-paced corporate environment that I was fully immersed in.

A couple of realities stood out to me: one was the connection between collaboration and success. I thrived in a collaborative environment, so that was exciting to me. But I also realized that there must be a welcome space within that environment for me to confidently engage and be embraced to collaborate. Then there was the second reality, which was not so exciting: the unspoken competitive nature of corporate culture. My peer group at work consisted of very motivated, confident people who operated with clearly defined visions for moving up the corporate ladder. I felt I was already at a disadvantage because I was battling beliefs that were impacting my confidence. I had to teach myself how to begin shedding or tailoring those beliefs that were clearly at odds with positioning myself professionally. I witnessed many others, who didn't look like me, seamlessly glide through opportunities and promotions. Why was I not experiencing that same level of ease or confidence? I wanted to glide, too.

Cultural Collisions

Why is she here? Does she even belong here? These are questions you probably never want anyone asking about you, but they were certainly asked about me. I joined Accenture in 1986, and over the years, I have heard many of my colleagues say, "If I had to interview today for a job at Accenture, I probably would not pass." It is a compliment to all of the amazing talent arriving at the organization nowadays. I always find that comment humorous, though, because I know, without a doubt, that I would not pass an interview today the way I showed up to mine all those years ago.

It was through the advocacy of an amazing woman, Marie Mann, that I began my journey with Accenture. Marie had been exposed to my work ethic—instilled in me by my parents—at the NYU Graduate School Office of Career Services during my co-op program. After my first promotion, I earned another promotion to Recruitment Coordinator. So there was no doubt in Marie's mind that I could successfully handle a similar position in a corporate setting where she was now an executive. Her belief in me taught me the power of unequivocal advocacy and the role we all can play.

I totally bombed my interview with the hiring partner. He was a tall white man, sharply dressed. He motioned me towards the sitting area of his very impressive corner office with large windows that let in the beautiful bright sunlight. It felt good to be in such an impressive space. My dad used to tell me about looking out of his work window and seeing the lights from the Wall Street office buildings shutting off at night. He told me of his hopes that his daughters could one day work in one of those office buildings. Now I was standing in an office that was more impressive than my father could have probably ever imagined.

When the partner asked what I knew about the firm, a standard interview question, my response was, "It's a bigeight accounting firm." (At the time, Accenture was known as Arthur Andersen.)

He followed up by asking what else I wanted to share. "Nothing," I replied with a smile that said, "That's all I know." But behind that smile, there was a lot of turmoil.

There was so much going on in my life personally—I was in a dysfunctional marriage, had a one-year-old daughter, and I'd just been laid off due to a bank merger—that I didn't have the capacity to give significant thought to what this interview could mean for me professionally. I showed up unprepared and clueless about how showing up that way could negatively impact my getting the job. It was an unimpressive interview to say the least. As I walked out, the partner handed me a company brochure and told me to read it for when we connected again. I took the brochure and in a very nonchalant manner responded, "Sure. No problem," as if I was speaking to a friend.

Years later, Marie confided in me that the partner had significant reservations about hiring me, but she believed in me and insisted that he give me the opportunity. After all, I was not the traditional profile candidate, and I had several strikes against me—I was still in the process of completing my bachelor's degree and going to school nights and weekends, I was attending a city college, which definitely was not one of the firm's target schools, and I was a Latina, not to mention that lackluster interview! But even with all of those strikes, what I did have was an advocate who admired my work ethic, recognized my value, and spoke up for me. She provided an opportunity that presented me with a choice to embrace it. That is the power of advocacy. Imagine showing up like that for people in your own sphere of influence.

Everything I've accomplished at Accenture started with that moment. Looking back, I recognize that Marie's advocacy propelled a career that ultimately impacted thousands of people around the globe. I did not fit the standard preferred profile back then because my credentials did not match their criteria. I was clearly not the right fit. Yet I went on to make significant contributions for so many people across multiple segments of diversity. The organization gave me the opportunity, and I delivered on it.

Organizations need to challenge themselves to evolve their recruitment strategies and go beyond their traditional hiring sources to reach additional skillful yet untapped talent. As they welcome that talent, they must reshape the culture to create an environment where those who pursued a different educational path do not feel inadequate, thereby intensifying their imposter syndrome. This is inclusive of candidates who pursued technical certifications or other skill-building paths instead of attending preferred top four-year college institutions. Organizations must then choose to retain the talent by providing opportunities to embrace, develop, and promote.

Belonging

My stylish entrance into the organization certainly exacerbated the questions of my belonging. I wore a bright tangerine satin suit with six huge gold buttons, styled with a pair of gold hoop earrings that were so big they hit my cheeks when I shook my head from side to side. I completed the look with a lipstick that was red-orange, and a pair of patent leather black, yellow, and orange stiletto shoes. Clearly, I knew how to coordinate! I walked into the human resources department on that first day fashionably late and feeling fabulous. Everyone was already settled in by the time I arrived, and I immediately captured their attention. I was obviously thinking that I looked so good, until the partner who hired me said, "Nellie, you look like the curtains in my living room." Without missing a beat, I responded with my quick wit and Bronx flavor, "Well, those must be some fabulous curtains." But as soon as I finished my statement, I noticed that I was the only pop of color in a dreary room of gray walls and navy suits. That was the beginning of my realization that I had just entered a conservative corporate world with which I was not familiar, a world where I was different, and I would have to figure out how to belong.

My introduction to the corporate environment came with many eye-opening firsts. Although I had previously worked in a bank, it was a junior administrative role where I was surrounded by many colleagues who were also people of color. The majority of the executive level was made up of white people, and it never crossed my mind to question why there were very few people of color in those roles. But it soon became all too overwhelming to be the only visible Latina within my new surroundings. I felt like an outsider on so many levels. It was my hairstyle, my clothes, and the way I sounded. Colleagues and leaders were constantly talking over me and taking the liberty to repeat what I had said, assuming others could not understand me, with a barrage of "What she is trying to say is . . ." or "What she means is . . ." I realized that my accent was an indicator to others about how they judged my level of intelligence, or lack thereof. I was dealing with an atmosphere in which I was constantly reminded of all my differences. Very early on, someone said to me, "You know, you're the first Latina hire here." To this day, I don't know if that was accurate, but I do know that statement propelled me to demonstrate how incredibly talented Latina women are.

When we, as people of color, find ourselves in these situations, we must start with the mindset of how we're going to respond.

We must tap into the grit and resilience we know we have. We should remind ourselves of the value we know we can add. And, more importantly, we should make an agreement with ourselves that we will not give others the power to determine the pace of our success. It's the choice to control the narrative we feed ourselves. The other choice is to minimize ourselves and rob ourselves of successes we know we otherwise can achieve. Choose you and the power of you, even when external forces are daring you to cave in. Not everything will be under our control, but for sure the way we choose to react most certainly is ours to navigate.

Prejudice and Racism in the Workplace

Throughout our corporate journeys, some of us may go through things that are hurtful and concerning, but some experiences cut us so deep that no matter how much we have evolved from them, the wound remains. I was walking by the secretarial bank one day when one of the assistants stopped me and handed me a subway token. She said, "Take this because you know you're the token hire here." I felt incredibly uncomfortable, but instead of acting on my feelings, I looked at the token and then I looked back at her. I chose to use humor in that moment because I wasn't going to show up as an angry Latina from the Bronx. "Well, they've hired the shiniest token," I said, meaning that if that's what I was, then they got the best of the best. Then I laughed and walked away. I could not give her the pleasure of knowing that she had offended or diminished me, so I leveraged humor as a way to protect my pride—something I did a lot in those first months. I think back on that now and question whether humor was the right approach. But up to that point, it was my protective shield and it worked for me. And by the way, I for sure took that token and used it for my train ride home, compliments of Miss Thang.

Another very painful incident occurred during a holiday party where the partner who hired me approached me with an impeccably wrapped gift. It had glittering white and red wrapping paper that looked like a sparkling candy cane, and I was so impressed when he handed it to me. I had only been in the organization for three months at the time and I was extremely excited about my first corporate holiday party. My colleagues had talked about how much fun the parties were, so I had been looking forward to it for weeks. I excitedly opened the gift to find a can of roach spray. Then he said, "We know that all Puerto Ricans have roaches in their homes." I was mortified. I wanted so badly to cry, but I couldn't let that happen in front of him and all of those laughing faces. I felt lightheaded and everyone looked blurry through the tears that welled in my eyes. But before they could run down my face, I pulled myself together, got up, and left. No one walked after me to ask if I was okay. I don't think anyone realized how offensive that gesture was. I was so upset that I cried the entire weekend. I didn't tell anyone in my family or group of friends what happened because I was too embarrassed. However, I did make the difficult choice not to let it go.

I decided to address the situation with courage, carefully plotting every word I would use. Standing in front of the mirror, I rehearsed all aspects of what I would say, down to the places where I would smile to soften the conversation and what hand gestures I would make. I wanted to make sure that I maintained control of my emotions.

I went back into work on Monday and headed straight for the partner's office, ready to deliver my entire speech. It was a much different experience from only three months earlier when I stood in that office for my interview. This time, I was sitting directly across from his beautiful, massive dark brown desk, not in his office sitting area. Sitting across from him, my heart beating very fast and tension building in my jaw, I forgot everything that I had rehearsed. So I just let go of the plan and spoke from my heart to explain how incredibly hurtful his actions were to me. Surprisingly, I was able to hold back my tears. His facial expression spoke volumes: I could see the embarrassment and his remorse. He looked intently into my eyes as I spoke, and I felt heard. I believed that the partner was genuinely apologetic. I told him that I didn't think I belonged in the organization, to which he responded, "Nellie, if you leave, you may potentially face these same issues elsewhere. If you stay, I will help you change this culture."

While what he did to me was extremely offensive, I felt a responsibility to educate in that moment. I chose empathy because I wholeheartedly believed that he had no idea how extremely hurtful that incident was, because I was probably the first person ever to call him on his behavior. I started to understand that I was going to face a lot of these moments where I would have to be the educator, and I had to be okay with it. I decided that I did not want others to experience what I had gone through during those three months. I know this may sound concerning or unacceptable in today's environment because, as people of color, the responsibility to educate should not sit solely with us. We need others to choose to be on this journey with us. But it was 1986 and those types of offensive actions were woven into the corporate culture. There was no accountability to be more thoughtful or inclusive. Today's employees have the ability to research the organizations to which they are going to align their talents and skills in a more informative way, including doing their research about how that brand aligns with diversity, inclusion, and equality. As people of color, we have more options now to align ourselves with brands that value us, and we must leverage that.

That uncomfortable incident was a pivotal moment in my career and the initial stages of building the brand of courage that I exhibit today. When faced with these unpleasant realities, I have had to stop and ask myself whether people are being intentionally hurtful or ignorantly hurtful, because there is a significant difference: someone we perceive as intentionally hurtful may have already established themselves as a person who demonstrates non-inclusive behavior. Someone we perceive as ignorantly hurtful may take us by surprise because their behavior feels unexpected and out of character. While there is a significant difference, it's not always clear because we each experience the impact through our own emotions and personal understanding.

Some people will respond positively to being educated while others will choose to resist the lesson and hold tight to their hurtful beliefs. On numerous occasions, I've had to decide whether to give individuals grace in the moment or recognize that the behavior needed to be immediately addressed. The thought process has to be quick: Should I address this? Is now the right time? How will this impact me or my career? However, the most important question I have asked myself is: Would I be okay with not addressing this and have this behavior impact someone else by my lack of inaction? The answer for me has always been super-clear: no. I personally believe in the power of sitting down and having courageous conversations with people about tough topics related to differences and diversity. My experience has been that, while some of these conversations are very uncomfortable, they are also necessary for people to evolve. I have found that when I have done this with courage and good intention, the outcome has always been one I am proud of. How can we expect people to create an environment of belonging for everyone if we are not providing the space for people to evolve, grow, and learn about others' identities and cultures? We simply cannot expect belonging without education and awareness.

The inner turmoil of that holiday party never went away. I remember the first time I shared the story on stage, I felt my lips quivering and I had to literally hold back my tears. It's gotten easier to share over the years, but some pain points remain raw for a lifetime.

The cultural collision that was my wardrobe persisted after my first day of work. I started paying attention to what other women in the office were wearing. They mostly wore navy blue skirt suits and dresses, or pale soft colors. I saw that a few of the women in my department favored the Laura Ashley brand, so I was determined to get a Laura Ashley dress. I found one and forced myself to try to like it.

It was pale pink (yuck) with an embroidered white collar and two white buttons. I put it on and immediately knew it wasn't me, but I wore it to the office because I was so desperately trying to fit in with everybody else. I went through the entire day incredibly uncomfortable and unable to show up authentically. I quickly discovered the power of my style and how deeply trying to embrace another style negatively affected my confidence. For me to show up as someone that I was not really affected me. I was not someone who wore pale pink dresses—the style did not represent me. I was not comfortable in my own skin that day, and it impacted how I was delivering and working. I felt horrible, like I had betrayed myself. I wondered how I could have allowed myself to feed into a narrative that I needed to change myself to fit in. I remember thinking that night that if I couldn't really be who I am, then no one will experience me at my best.

That day, I learned the importance of being authentic, which is something I'd never thought about until I had tried hard to be like somebody else. I decided that, although I could make some adjustments to how I was showing up, I could not do it at the expense of my full authenticity. I never wore that pale pink Laura Ashley dress ever again. What I did wear was a bright pink winter coat and matching snow boots. Once again, the partner who hired me decided to voice his opinion, telling me that I looked like the Easter Bunny in that coat. I thought, "This is comical. First I look like your curtains and now I'm the Easter Bunny." Through those types of comments, I realized that maybe he had a point. I had to find a balance between adjusting to the company's culture at the time and maintaining my own style. While I didn't want to be someone else, my wardrobe did start getting darker. The orange and pink were replaced with brown, black, navy, and gray. But I always adorned those neutral suits with flashy jewelry or colorful shoes. I am glad we have evolved as a corporate culture to a place where people have the opportunity to express themselves through their own personal and unique styles, and I like to think that I have been part of that change.

As a Latina, I am all too familiar with the codeswitching I need to perform across multiple settings. I have always been very careful about how it is impacting my comfort level. Does it sometimes feel like too much of a compromise, too much of a stretch, or requiring too much energy? It is hard layering all of the filters required simply to feel some sense of belonging. However, it is harder to feel good about yourself when you feel inauthentic.

Defining Moments

"You were way too animated." "You came across too flat and dry." These are two very opposing pieces of feedback. Yet it's common feedback when people of color are presenting in front of nondiverse teams. Either our expressive style and excitement is perceived as too over the top, or we suppress all that flavorful personality and end up being criticized for a low-energy presentation. This type of feedback related to a style bias remains a reality today. In one recent conversation, a young Latino from a technology organization said to me, "I want to change the way my team is presenting our products to our customers and clients to make them more appealing and relatable. I spent days preparing for my presentation, adding innovative ways to present our offerings, tapping into my creativity and cultural savvy. I was really getting into my presentation; I was so excited! But after, not one leader commented on the content of the presentation; instead they each homed in on my style and their obvious discomfort with it." The feedback left him feeling deflated and questioning whether he belonged. He wondered how damaging that presentation would be to his career and whether he had taken too big a risk by being himself.

These types of experiences are defining moments in a person's career journey. You can choose to push through and continue to effect change with the intent to evolve the brand and culture (like when I remained genuine to myself by adding flair to my wardrobe), or you choose to stay within the existing flow, limiting your drive and robotically putting forth all of you into your deliverables. If you choose the latter, the organization does not get the best of you, or you ultimately leave out of frustration.

In a conversation I had with a banking executive, she characterized people of color, including herself, as sensitive. I immediately rectified that statement. I told her that it is not that we are sensitive; it is that our sensitivities are heightened due to our lived experiences combatting biases that continue to accumulate, leaving us heedful and measured as we navigate through the corporate culture. Of course we are going to be deliberate about examining and evaluating the experiences we are having with others. Of course it would be prudent to consider what biases are playing out for us. Of course this all would spark a predisposition to be doubtful. And of course, all of this energy is draining and exhausting.

Early on in my career, I self-appointed myself to be the change agent. I decided that I would have a big influence in evolving the company culture. As such, speaking up and being the voice of change became a daily mission for me. I remember one particular conference call where I found myself questioning whether I pushed too hard yet again to insert my thoughts about the lack of diversity. I was feeling the heaviness of having to highlight the same issues over and over, like a rinse-and-repeat conversation. I felt like people were tuning me out, and in a fleeting moment I started to question whether I should scale back. I reached out to my leader and said, "I feel like I am always the one bringing up the need to increase our diversity. Today I feel like people are just tired of hearing me."

His response became a message that I would repeat over and over to myself whenever I was in doubt about my role and impact. He said, "Nellie, the day you stop showing up to these meetings insisting on cultural change, that is the day you stop doing right by our organization and by what you are destined to accomplish." *Wow*—there was so much power within those words. Empowerment comes from within, but some of it can also be influenced by those around you. Just the fact that I was willing to be vulnerable (which did not come easy for me) and share my feelings with him was a sign that we were transitioning to a mentoring relationship. He saw the power of me. I experienced his willingness to listen and acknowledge the importance of what I was doing, and we both grew from that moment.

That was the day that I decided that we needed to bring together the few executive African American and Hispanic American leaders we had at the time. I wanted us together in a room discussing ways in which we were going to increase our representation. I reached out to each individually, set the date, set the agenda, and set out to infuse urgency to my goal and bring others along who would have a vested interest. That was the beginning of experiencing the power and impact of relatability with colleagues who get you!

Speak Up for Yourself

After a couple of years within the organization, I found myself conflicted between not asking for too much from my leader and not leaving anything to chance or luck. I decided to dismiss the former to focus instead on the latter and put a plan to get a promotion into effect. On the day that I put my plan into action I felt exhilaration. But riding the bus to my parent's house for dinner, I also had deep concerns knowing that I had just made a bold move.

As I stepped out of the elevator, I was immediately taken by the flavorful aroma of sofrito. No one could beat my mom at cooking

pollo guisado (chicken stew). I picked up my daughter and placed
her on my lap, and said, "Guess what Mami did today finally?"

She replied with a childish sass, "You went to work and came back."

"Yes, I went to work and I did something big," I said, trying to
build the excitement around my announcement. "I asked my
boss for a promotion! Yay!" My toddler daughter had no idea
what a promotion meant, but she followed my celebratory cues
and began to clap and laugh joyfully. My mom, on the other
hand, turned towards me with a concerned look on her face.

"Ay, Dios mio, Nellie, why did you that do? Didn't you tell me
that you think your boss suffers from ulcers? You for sure just
made that man's ulcer worse today."

"Ay, Mami," I responded. "If I don't look out for myself and insist
on being acknowledged, then I am for sure going to get an ulcer
myself. I can't keep watching others getting promoted and not me.
One of my team members, Kim, just got promoted. She was hired
after me and now she is above me and her parents announced her
promotion in the town paper. Who even knew that was a thing?"

My dad slowly placed his fork down and calmly chimed in, "Well,
Nellie, let's hope that this didn't make him feel like you are now
becoming a burden for him."

My parents couldn't fathom asking for a raise. Their wages were
always dictated for them. I was stepping out of their familiar
comfort zone and that disconnect was playing out in front of me.
The conviction, independence, and courage they had instilled in
me throughout my life was at odds with the concern they were
showcasing now. It was a dinner conversation that remains vivid

in my mind to this day. Reflecting on it now, I have no doubt in my mind that it would have played out much differently for a person whose parents already knew how to navigate corporate America. That conversation probably would have been all about advice for effectively asking for a promotion and a raise.

I once heard a leader of color say, "My conversations over dinner with my parents were never about how to be successful in the business world. They were more about our struggles in facing and dealing with racism and our history. While these are all vital lessons, their exclusivity can potentially narrow our ability to proactively navigate the corporate environment. I didn't get the insights to give me a good head start." Access to insight is powerful.

Kim, who got promoted over me, had done a great job at networking with company leaders. She always oozed confidence. She seemed to fit in perfectly, not burdened by the biases related to people of color. I watched her come in and effortlessly claim her space in an environment designed for people like her to succeed. I was really mad and quite frankly jealous, but I had to quickly reevaluate my perspective. I had to admit that Kim had been doing the work. Yes, she fit the mold, but she was also extremely personable, and she knew how to successfully rally around leaders and build valuable relationships within the firm.

When seeking that first promotion, I was driven solely by emotion and what I perceived as lack of fairness. I started the conversation with "Help me understand why I have not been promoted." I had no insight into how these types of conversations should be approached.

Over the years, I learned the more effective way to position myself for continued growth and opportunities within an organization. I understood that leadership wouldn't position me for promotions; instead I needed to do it for myself. I knew that when I did, I had to be clear about why I merited that promotion, letting them know exactly how I'd delivered and why I deserved recognition.

You have to ask yourself a few questions:

- Are you in a role that warrants a promotion and has been designated for growth?
- Have you showcased the skills, value, and impact expected within the role?
- Is there someone who is sponsoring or advocating for you?

If the answer is no to any of these, the speed by which you reach the next level will be impacted. In relation to those questions, consider these elements:

- Assess your current skill set. Is it aligned to where the growth of the business is heading?
- Ask yourself if you gravitate toward new roles, or tend to stay stuck in a role with no further room for growth.
- Take inventory of your network. Are there influencers and sponsors within your group you can tap into?

When others get promoted around you, you can choose to get mad and envious, or you can choose to find out what that person did to get that promotion before you and identify what you need to do to better position yourself for the next one. I made a choice not to be mad at Kim, but instead focused my attention on what I needed to do in my career both to advance myself and to change the culture. If I had placed all of my energy on being angry with

Kim, I would have diminished my personal opportunity to do better and rise within the organization. Instead, I chose to align my focus and energy intentionally on how to attract and mentor diverse talent, educate leaders in increasing their awareness related to bias and gaps, and insert my DE&I role in performance and promotion discussions. I was also going to take control and visibly position myself.

Waiting for Permission

Did I ask for permission? Did I get the permission? Who gave me the permission? At what point do we stop asking these three questions in our professional lives? When working within the corporate environment, many people of color show up waiting for permission to claim their space or waiting to be told that we have power. We have trepidation about negotiating and advocating for what we have earned. I feel that the younger generation does a better job of advocating for themselves today, but they still face some challenges. Even in my own career, I know that I missed opportunities along the way because I failed to recognize my power earlier on, or I failed to put the power I had attained into effect.

People of color show up as if we have to be perfect 110% of the time because we feel an extra layer of responsibility to prove ourselves. But we don't shake that off early enough in our careers. When we reach the levels of leaders and executives, we are expected to make decisions without constantly consulting our own leadership. When we fail to take enough risk on our own and to confidently lead, we become those executives who fail to add value independently and position ourselves effectively.

The performance review experience offers an example of how waiting for permission can impact us early in our career journey. When sitting in a review, are you waiting for permission to advocate for yourself, or are you taking the initiative to fully benefit from that time with your leader? If you aren't asking the following questions, you are probably waiting for permission:

- How am I doing against my objectives?
- What can I do to expand my scope in order to reach the next level?
- What leadership exposure do I need aside from my sponsors and advocates?

These may sound like a given, but it can be incredibly challenging for some people to ask these very direct questions. If you are not asking them, you aren't getting the feedback you need to ensure that you will reach that next level. Even when a leader says you are doing great, it may feel good to hear, but if that is all you receive from the leader, you have been dealt a great disservice. People push back when I say this, but it is within our own power to ensure that our performance evaluation conversations are effective and valuable. If the leader is not comfortable giving feedback, then it is up to you to ask the necessary questions. Getting to a place of belonging also requires representing ourselves and asking the tough questions that help us position ourselves to evolve. We have to own some of that belonging. People often say, "Well, it's not up to me to change the culture." But it's up to all of us. Everybody plays a part.

We have to be active participants in our own advocacy, which in a corporate setting also includes paying attention to our surroundings. When I am in a room, I am paying attention to who is connecting with whom. I'm paying attention to who is ignoring me. I'm paying attention to who is dismissing my contributions and who is recognizing my value. By paying attention to all of these things, I gain an advantage in recognizing who wants to see me succeed and who does not. Part of chasing belonging is identifying the people who make you feel like you belong. Who are the ones welcoming you and embracing you? And for the ones who are not, what do you choose to do or not do about it? Ask yourself, what impact can this person have on your career? Does it matter, and why? It is all part of being strategic and intentional about your professional journey.

At a very junior time in my career, I attended a recruiter's conference where our CEO at the time was going to speak. As I entered the auditorium, I noticed where he was sitting and made a beeline over to sit behind him. I spoke to him in a very intentional manner to ensure that he acknowledged my presence. When he went up on stage to speak, he said, "I want to ask the recruiters a question. Nellie, come on up here." I could hear my colleagues buzzing about the CEO knowing my name and calling me on stage. It was a defining moment for me. But had I not paid attention to my surroundings to sit strategically behind him and speak to him, it would never have happened.

So, what does a sense of belonging look and feel like to me? It's a space where I feel safe and I interpret others in the room to be welcoming of me, where I can let my guard down and feel at ease.

When employees of color work within a corporate culture where they do not feel seen, chances are they have not been placed in roles designed for promotion. They also probably don't have advocates speaking out on their behalf. When I think about my own journey, I reflect on how I created and evolved my role and promotions. There was no diversity role at Accenture at the time, and no established blueprint for one. I created and evolved it. I was consistently asking myself, "How do I position myself? How do I demonstrate the value? How do I continuously increase my skillset? What leader do I align with?" I had to be creative and intentional about how I was going to show up. What has always worked for me is having the courage to ask. I had to be willing to tell my story and advocate for myself. Junior in my career, I was asked by a leader why getting a promotion was so important to me. I responded, "Because I earned it and it will increase the credibility of my diversity role." I recognized that the promotion was bigger than me. It was about elevating the role of diversity within the organization.

What It's Like to Experience Belonging

Chasing belonging has played out differently throughout my corporate journey, as it has and will in yours as well. When you start a new role and you're embarking on your career, there's nervous energy and excitement. You may question yourself and experience a lot of doubt, but you must be able to assess the landscape that you've entered. Early on in my career, it was the colorful comparisons to curtains and offensive gifts and actions that clearly added to the challenges of the environment. During one of my other early attempts for advancement in my career, I asked my lead for a promotion. He responded by asking how old my daughter was. When I said that she was two, he replied, "They need you so much during that age, I am sure all of your energy needs to go there." Was he discouraging me from pursuing the promotion because I devote a lot of time and energy to my young daughter, or was he simply being thoughtful? Did he make other discouraging comments to my peers who were not mothers? It's those types of subtle biases and behaviors that shake your confidence and leave you questioning yourself. I felt like I could no longer freely talk about my daughter around him out of my concern that he might leverage it as a disadvantage to my career.

So what does a sense of belonging look and feel like to me? It's a space where I feel safe and I interpret others in the room to be welcoming of me, where I can let my guard down and feel at ease. I can relate to people better. I am not constantly decoding verbal and nonverbal cues. My experience is not overcome by needing to put significant effort into finding a way to fit in and feel welcomed or valued. Now, imagine if you could experience belonging every day. Your engagement and contributions to your company, and your own success, would be unstoppable. This is exactly why organizations should be looking at belonging as a critical component of their business-driven strategies.

Questions for Consideration

1. What have been your cultural collisions in your professional life? How have they worked to your disadvantage or advantage?

2. What incidents or experiences do you need to let go of that are weighing you down?

3. How are you courageously leveraging your voice to advocate for yourself and to amplify the voices of others?

2

The Constant Work Against Marginalization

What's working for me? What's not working for me? What needs to work for me? I have consistently asked myself these three crucial questions throughout my career to prompt an important internal dialogue and bring about clarity for myself, fully recognizing that I am the only one who has the responsibility and power to provide the answers. It is foolish to give your responsibility and power away for others to decide what works for you. They can make recommendations, share assumptions, and even exhibit some level of influence over what they believe is the right path for you, but only you know what is in your best interest. These three questions have helped me work through the complexities of what I needed in those moments when I have felt marginalized. They have also propelled me to incredible new heights, because working through each answer has guided me to intentionally redirect or realign when necessary to shape and achieve my goals.

In school, many of us experienced bullying in one form or another. Some people did the bullying and others were bullied. Even if we were not the ones personally involved, we likely witnessed the level of pain and hurt that a bully can evoke. These menacing behaviors strip away our right to be fearless and stifle our ability to be carefree, daring, nervy, and bodacious. While most of us do not talk about bullying as adults within the corporate culture, we do commonly experience its effects when people intentionally, with their words and actions, seek to make other people feel marginalized. We know an environment of acceptance promotes feelings of security, enabling us to uninhibitedly shape who we can potentially become. An environment riddled with marginalization has the opposite effect, and many will agree that it disproportionately impacts diverse groups across industries. It often happens in subtle ways, but those microinequities continuously add up until they become undeniable to the person on the receiving end. Microinequities hinder our potential and credibility, limiting our ability to fully contribute to the workspace.

During a conversation about marginalization with a woman of color in a senior position, she said in a reflective tone, "I bet there have been so many times that I have gone through it and haven't called it what it actually is. Instead, I convince myself that I am exaggerating or being overly sensitive." This is such a common sentiment. No one wants to be labeled overly sensitive or an exaggerator. Despite feeling the effects of marginalization, we constantly justify these behaviors with all of the different reasons why it is not actually happening. These incidents begin to make us question ourselves. They plant those pesky seeds of doubt, making us feel unsure of our abilities. Our automatic response is to assume that it is all in our heads, but through an accumulation of these moments and experiences, we begin to feel the effects more intently and come to a disheartening realization: "Yup, I am being marginalized." It may take some people a while to recognize what's happening to them, but for others that realization comes much more quickly.

Marginalization in Action

Marginalization shows up in a lot of different ways for professionals of color. When we are the last to be selected or never selected for a role or project, even though we clearly have the skills to excel in it. When we are constantly interrupted when speaking or presenting. When we are the only ones on a call not receiving compliments or acknowledgment. When we are never referenced by name because team members, colleagues, or leaders have not taken the time to ask how to pronounce it. Infuriatingly, we are marginalized when leaders know we are good at what we do choose not to trust that we are good enough: "Well, let me run your ideas by a couple of other people." While some do this with complete awareness of their bias about people of color, others are subconsciously conditioned to believe that people of color are not as capable or intelligent. In both cases, validating someone's work or ideas through others who represent familiarity, or a positive bias, becomes their default. They choose to go to the people with whom they comfortably align and feel that they can 100% trust or the people for whom they have a higher regard.

Marginalization also shows up within one-on-one interactions where leaders insist on multitasking instead of focusing on the communication at hand, deeming you not important or critical enough to receive their undivided attention. Admittedly, leaders—and people in general—have some calls that they look forward to and some calls that they dread getting on. We're human; it happens. But when diverse people show up to a call with a leader who does not reflect their diversity, we bring a cautious perspective to the experience. As such, when our attempts at communication are met by a leader who is simultaneously responding to messages or checking a phone, it presents, yet again, as one of the many exclusionary behaviors we face in our journeys.

Most leaders would say that they do not intentionally set out to make people feel marginalized. Leaders often have multiple competing priorities, and they may not realize how splitting their focus can negatively impact their teams. I once had a new team member based out of India who needed onboarding, and she had reached out to me urgently. I had been traveling internationally, and I was tired, sleep deprived, and had only enough energy to devote to the most urgent priorities, let alone onboarding a new team member. I chose different priorities, but when I realized how marginalizing that might have felt for her, I immediately stopped in my tracks and called her, determined to give her the undivided attention that she deserved.

Before diving into my apology and reasons, I decided to give her the opportunity to express her feelings and emotions. She said, "Nellie, in order for me to do my job, I need to have clarity about your direction and expected timeline." She gave me a reminder about the importance of putting team members first and I appreciated her assertiveness. I apologized to her and shared the reasons for my not reaching out sooner. I felt that I owed her an explanation because I recognized the strong possibility that she might have felt marginalized as a person on the team who was not receiving the responsiveness that others were and what she needed at the time. As leaders, we need to hold ourselves accountable to recognize when our actions or choices may result in team members feeling devalued.

Another marginalizing scenario that I've seen play out is when a person of color speaks up during a meeting and nobody responds or agrees, or even acknowledges that the person spoke up. I remember being on a sizable executive team call where only two of us were people of color. The other person was from Latin America and had what some people in the meeting perceived as a thick accent. During the call, he made a recommendation, and no one in this generally chatty group said a word, not even the leader of the committee. This was a person in a leadership role speaking out in a meeting and getting zero response. The silence was uncomfortable, and it resonated with me. It was a feeling that I had experienced many times myself. You start to nervously wonder if you were disconnected and lost everyone on the call or if you had been speaking on mute. You almost hope that it was one of the above and not that you were just completely ignored or dismissed.

The loud silence motivated me to step in and say, "Thank you for sharing your idea with the group. It aligns nicely with the organizational goals discussed earlier." That may seem like a simple statement, but it was actually loaded with intention: acknowledgment, validation, and action. First and foremost, I stepped in so he could feel acknowledged. Then I had to affirm my positive reaction to his suggestion in order to publicly validate it. Finally, I had to encourage action from the group by tying the idea to goals shared earlier. After the call ended, he reached out to thank me for speaking out and acknowledging him. True to my brand, I once again made a decision to educate and reached out to the committee lead. I started the conversation by letting her know that my goal in reaching out to her was to create greater awareness and help her evolve as an inclusive leader. I then said to her, "It took a woman of color to acknowledge a man of color." She responded, "Oh my gosh, Nellie! I promise you that I didn't even think of it that way." I believed her and replied, "This is where the opportunities show up for leaders to learn, evolve, and commit to creating an inclusive environment."

Having to navigate through these microaggressions and microinequities is a distraction too real and impossible to ignore.

I have hundreds of conversations with people across multiple organizations and many of those conversations stick with me. They fuel me to continue courageously evoking cultural change across industries. During a conversation with one such talented woman of color, she said, "On my way out of my previous employer, I decided to tell leadership my story and share how I had been negatively impacted throughout my tenure. There weren't many overt offensive moments, but rather too many subtle moments of marginalization to count. I had nothing to lose at that moment. As it was all flowing out, I began to feel lighter, liberated with an ease that was unfamiliar to me." She continued, "Nellie, imagine how amazing it must be for those who don't have to carry the load we carry or need to navigate the hidden dangers of bias we do. They have the benefit and ease of simply having to focus on the work at hand."

Though it can be tricky to categorize due to the many dynamics playing out within a team environment, the interruption experience can also be associated with marginalization. There is a sense that people of color get interrupted or dismissed at a higher rate than others. I recall the experience of an executive woman of color who was on a call with a group of leaders when one of her colleagues continuously interrupted her. He wasn't interrupting anybody else. It took another woman to call him out on it for him to apologize to his colleague. He said that he didn't even realize that he was doing it, but it was obvious to several people that there was an unconscious bias guiding his behavior. Unconscious biases influence our decisions and behaviors in subtle ways; so much so that they can completely escape our notice. They are a product of culture, family influence, or life experiences. This is what so many diverse people encounter, and what nondiverse leaders and colleagues need to understand. Having to navigate through these microaggressions and microinequities is a distraction too real and impossible to ignore.

Comfort Zone for Whom?

The actions of leaders can bring up feelings of marginalization in so many ways, and group meetings provide a perfect illustration. While waiting for a meeting to start, team members typically begin with smalltalk, or what I refer to as "warm-up" conversations. These may seem insignificant, but just as warming up to play a sport is necessary for best performance output, warm-up conversations can set the stage for impactful contributions to the meeting. You are empowered by the confidence boost you get when you have already talked or laughed with other participants.

So many times, I have watched leaders across multiple organizations enter a room prior to a meeting and change the dynamic of these warm-up conversations by immediately going over to acknowledge their go-to people, while excluding others in the room. When this occurs, that leader has done two things. First, they have demonstrated to everybody in the room that those are their "chosen" people. Second, they just empowered those people to show up more relaxed and take more risks by giving them the confidence boost that naturally comes with being acknowledged. At the same time, those few minutes of selective interaction may have just negatively impacted someone else for the entire meeting. For some leaders, these behaviors occur unintentionally, while others strategically leverage these moments to reconfirm whom they are selectively dismissing and whom they have chosen as their go-to people.

When I do trainings about creating an inclusive culture across various organizations and industries, I ask leaders to think about the previous year and all of the great projects they've led. Looking around the room, I'll see smiles and looks of satisfaction. I then ask them to think about the people they have included in those projects. The smiles continue. Then I ask them to think about the people they consciously or unconsciously chose to leave out. The energy starts to shift. Finally, I ask them, "What do the people you left out look like? What groups do they represent?" Boom! The entire energy of the room changes because it is rare that they are asked about the people they left out. I eventually cut the tension by letting them know that I didn't ask them those questions to shame them. I asked the questions to help them change and evolve, as well as have them think about their responsibility towards equity. Are they being fair and impartial in choosing their teams? I prompt them to consider the following:

- How many legacy team members do you have? These are the people you have chosen to work with over an extended period of time, bringing them along as you climb the corporate ladder.

- How many team members are fairly new to you, or somewhat unfamiliar, but you decided to add them based on the skills required?

- What is the diversity representation on your team? Are you holding yourself accountable to be inclusive?

- What biases are you aware of within yourself and where do you have opportunity to evolve?

- How may your existing biases be impacting your decisions about whom you sponsor and advocate for?

Human nature is such that we automatically go to our comfort zones. This can be driven by how unconscious bias is formed and shaped through our experiences, socialization, and exposure to other views about groups of people. But awareness equals responsibility, which should guide us to step out of our comfort zones and evolve towards inclusion. Unless we do that, we're not going to solve for the lack of belonging that people experience within the corporate environment.

The Marginalization Effect

The effects of being marginalized lead to feeling devalued. I often see it play out. People gradually get so used to missing opportunities to be heard that they begin to shut down. The only way they will engage is when someone intentionally pulls them in. Let's go back to the meeting warm-up scenario. The reality is that, far too often, when diversity is not represented within a meeting setting, it reduces our comfort level significantly. We make the decision not to engage, which is often driven by factors such as these:

- Finding the warm-up small talk unrelatable
- Having an uncomfortable or unpleasant past experience with someone in the group
- Not being extroverted or expressive
- Feeling too junior or new to contribute comfortably
- Protecting yourself from potentially being dismissed or ignored
- Waiting for the perfect moment to politely insert yourself
- Not feeling the psychological safety to engage

Whenever I find myself in a situation where I choose not to engage in the warm-up chatter, it feels as though I have already started the meeting at a disadvantage. In that moment, I force myself to consider whether my lack of engagement stems from my being intentionally excluded, or if it is happening because my comfort level or interest were just not there. Having an awareness of the *why* is important to me and it drives how I choose to or need to show up for the remainder of the existing meeting, as well as future meetings.

When trying to determine whether I have placed my own blockers in the way, I consider these questions:

- Have I given too much importance and credence to those who have created a narrative or portrayal of me that is contradictory to my skills and abilities?
- Am I allowing a sense of defeat to negatively impact the energy level required to combat the damaging biases aimed at me?
- Have I placed a significant amount of blame on outside factors and bias narrative instead of what actions I own in the moment?
- Am I feeling intimidated?

So I ask you, are you using these warm-up conversations as an opportunity to engage? Some enter the room or videoconference call and effortlessly engage in these exchanges, while others sit in silence without making a single contribution. Is this happening to you?

Taking Back Your Power

If you are one of the people who doesn't get acknowledged by the leaders who walk into those rooms, it is time to make a decision. Yes, that happened, but now what? Are you going to let your energy be affected for the next several hours, or are you going to choose to claw your way into that conversation and get as well situated as the people who were addressed? It's hard when you've been put at a disadvantage in the first few minutes of a meeting, but we owe it to ourselves to choose to do something about it. We must find ways to engage.

I've been in situations where I am in a room listening to leaders laugh and talk about their country clubs, extravagant vacations, or golf games, while I sit there trying to figure out how to fit in. Yes, I've had a seat at the table, but I had to figure out how to really be heard. I had to ask myself what would not work for me, and the answer has always been not leveraging that seat, no matter how challenging the situation.

We must get into the mode of figuring out how we solve the problem. We have to make thoughtful choices. Consider these possible scenarios:

- If your recommendations and ideas are constantly shut down, but yet others with similar thoughts are embraced, ask why. Identify one or two people you can share your recommendation with and engage them in supporting your ideas; make them allies of your recommendations and ideas.

- If your name is mispronounced or simply not verbalized by those who have not taken the time to familiarize themselves with it, identify ways to change that. Talk to the individuals and send an email with your name phonetically indicated.

- If a leader, colleague, or peer takes credit for your work, turn that frustration or disappointment towards identifying what must be done differently next time and what must be done now to be acknowledged as a significant contributor. Ask for the project lead to provide written feedback for your contributions to be part of your performance review.

- When you feel marginalized, ask yourself: Am I okay with letting this go? How damaging can this be to me or those like me, if I don't address it? Do I need to engage others to help me solve for this?

As a woman of color with an accent, I understand the level of preparation that it takes to show up confidently and speak up. Early on in my career, whenever I was interrupted or dismissed, it drained my efforts to smoothly engage and confidently show up. Sometimes leaders and colleagues go into a call displaying a bias against accents. They don't want to intentionally put the effort into getting past the accent, and in many cases they completely disengage or interrupt abruptly and quite noticeably. Experiencing this behavior may position those of us with accents to shut down. But I challenge us not to! Our accents do not determine our abilities, intelligence, or expertise. They simply reflect the sounds of our beautiful cultures. We need to infuse pride into the way we sound, no matter what space or setting we find ourselves in. We own that decision. With that mind shift, we can stop giving so much attention to how we sound and instead focus on the content of what we are delivering.

I recognize that this mind shift can be difficult for some, but think of it this way: How much longer are you going to allow the way that you sound to hold you back from what you know you are 100% capable of accomplishing? Make the decision not to be held back by your accent by confidently speaking up and contributing to conversations. Those around you will eventually stop hearing the accent. As it becomes familiar to them, they will begin focusing on the content of your words. That's the power of shifting how we show up.

The Senior Level Is Not a Shield

Being a senior or executive leader does not make you immune from marginalization. Bias associated with your demographic group or diverse identity can show up at any time throughout your career. While you may have reached a place in your journey where you have become savvier about how to identify it, as well as how to respond to it, there still comes that moment or moments when you are surprised that bias has shown up in your space again. You once again need to deduce whether your interpretation of an incident is accurate.

I have never claimed to have the power to decipher someone else's intention, particularly when they are displaying biased behavior, and I cannot with complete conviction tell you if the bias exhibited was intentional or unintentional—even though I will certainly have my own opinions about it. However, as the recipient and the person impacted by the actions, I can with absolute certainty decide for myself when the behavior has resulted in making me feel belittled or marginalized. So when people casually try to dismiss the marginalization of any group with comments like "That can happen to anyone, not just to people of color," I calmly give this response: "I trust that the people impacted are wise and confident enough to know what has been displayed towards them." People sometimes want to classify the situation differently, giving it another meaning or making you question your personal interpretation. It may be that they are aiming to make you feel better, which can be nice and appreciated, or that they want to protect the person who displayed the behavior. Either way, the person impacted must be given the platform to share their truth about how they feel.

During a review session for a project, I expressed significant reservations to a colleague about an approach she was opting to take and I informed her I would not place my brand behind it if the team moved forward with the current design of the project. This was not an easy decision for me. I am known for collaborating, advocating, supporting, and lifting teams. It was the first time in my career that I ever refused to place my brand behind a project. It was also the first time I was so adamantly opposed to my colleague's direction. But that is how incredibly convinced I was that the direction was not right.

Despite my objections, she decided to test the project with a small group. When I learned about it, I was told that she wanted to get more opinions (hmm, this feels familiar). Two reactions soared through me. First, my expertise and leadership input obviously was not enough to convince her that it was the wrong direction, and that did not feel good. Second, I had to be open to her decision to pilot test the project. In my mind, I was confident that the results would confirm my opposition. As it turned out, the feedback was exactly as negative and concerning as I had predicted it would be.

While I felt validated, I did not spend any time gloating about my accurate prediction. Instead, I chose to quickly pivot. I had to think through what my role was in helping redirect one particular team member who was feeling deflated. Now, to be clear, choosing to do that did not take away from the fact that I was still feeling very dismissed by the experience. But here is the power of not letting ego enter the equation, having good intentions, and courageously engaging in productive conversations. I unapologetically communicated to my colleague how I was made to feel marginalized by her decision to ignore my direct feedback and so adamantly resist my recommendation. My direct message to her was, "If you have ever wondered how it is that women of color are made to feel belittled, unwelcome, pushed aside, and basically marginalized, then may I suggest you look no further than yourself. You have just exhibited those behaviors towards me."

A week later, she called me to apologize. She acknowledged that her actions were wrong, though she could offer no explanation as to why she had behaved that way. I listened and said, "Thank you for the apology. I appreciate it and deserve it." We both chuckled for a moment and then proceeded to have a lengthy conversation.

I am convinced that we were able to have this very necessary and transparent, uncomfortable, but productive conversation because we both showed up with the right spirit. We demonstrated our professional support of one another, ditched any potential judgment, and simply talked. This is how I choose to have impactful and necessary breakthroughs. Ignoring the behaviors or labeling them as something else does not address the issue or drive the change that needs to happen. Some people do not feel that they have the power to effect change within the corporate environment, but we have power at any level to speak up for ourselves and say what we choose not to accept. And there are many ways that we can do that. Choosing to ignore it is the one that requires less energy. It feels safer and less complicated, but it is the most damaging choice.

Questions for Consideration

1. How do you recognize when you're being marginalized?
2. In what ways might you be marginalizing others?
3. How do you confront marginalization?

Understand Your Power; Claim Your Worth

You got this! You earned this! Now claim your power! I turn to these affirmations, particularly when feeling that the bar has been raised, with new expectations set either by me or for me. They provide the internal guidance I need to adjust in a changing landscape. Too often, we fail to recognize the power that we have earned, so we do not fully leverage it.

I often get asked about the pivotal moment I unapologetically claimed my power. There are so many moments I can point to, but a few stand out as critical points in my career where I undoubtedly claimed my space. When we are determined to close gaps and solve for challenges plaguing diverse communities, we will find ourselves needing to tap into our innermost confidence to assert ourselves and effect change. Those actions associated with creating change will many times require the cooperation, agreement, and engagement of multiple leaders. These changes will require the disruption of the standard ways of doing things. They will require embedding new processes that generate additional work, which will cause some to hesitate or challenge the value of the new things being introduced.

Throughout my leadership I have introduced multiple new programmatic ways to solve for closing gaps. Many times I was tasked with bringing other leaders along to agree. Some of those conversations were pleasant and easy; others were extremely challenging. As I was introducing a process for increasing the internal progression of people of color, I was met with some resistance. I understood why, though. For the process to work, the leaders would have to get on a call with me to go over every single person within their own groups. They would also need to have a call with their HR leads to get familiar with their teams.

I was asking extremely busy leaders to focus more time and energy on something new. But I was confident that the process would set a tone by which the business leaders would begin to feel accountable for the diverse representation within their groups. It would encourage the responsibility for each to be more aware of the talent. Simply, we were asking the leaders to become familiar with various ethnic demographics at the executive level and above, and identify whether each was aligned to the right client, in the right role, and had the right sponsor (what we called the 3R Process Review). Yet I wouldn't give up, and kept insisting that these calls be put on the leaders' calendars. Still, the resistance remained high.

I made the decision to leverage my power by approaching the leaders who resisted the least and started with them. I also enlisted their HR leads to explain to them how the process was going to help them solve for closing a gap. Once I got some leaders on board, I had them explain to the other leaders how useful the exercise had been. My persistence was relentless, and they eventually became quarterly calls. It was quite impressive to see how these leaders evolved. Starting from the initial calls where there was only some familiarity with those within their groups, to witnessing the full-on awareness of the experience and positioning of each individual we identified, it was an evolution that proved impactful in creating the responsibility and accountability to solve for retaining, developing, and advancing the talent.

In moments like these, I needed to self-assess my own internal conversations and evaluate how they were influencing my outward actions so that I could lift my credibility for continued growth. How you see yourself is how you start to show up, and if we don't exude our power, others will not value it. We owe it to ourselves to conduct these self-assessments so that we can confront the negative thoughts before they manifest in our behaviors and the decisions we make. For instance, if we let a leader or peer intimidate us, in every subsequent interaction with that individual, we may show up in a passive way. We give up our power when worrying about others' perceptions about us and mentally editing every word before we vocalize it. But if we are mindful of that, we can change the narrative and show up very differently for those interactions.

Despite being intentional about staying positive and motivated, facing resistance is an unavoidable part of the professional journey. On many occasions, I faced the challenge of convincing others to embrace and prioritize my visions. I had to bring them along on the journey of my creative process while demonstrating the value of what I intended to achieve. It required me to adjust my approach in an effort to obtain the buy-in and sponsorship of key people who were crucial to my success and that of the program. I used these challenges as fuel to reach my goals.

When assessing if external factors are stifling your power, there are three key points to consider:

- Are you being left out of key meetings or discussions that would otherwise be appropriate for your level and role?
- Are facts that are important to your success being misrepresented or withheld?
- Are you continuously being forced into a box or typical role with limited ability for visibility, growth, and advancement?

Once you have answered those questions, consider these additional points for tapping into your own personal power and bringing others along to support your vision:

- Have you recognized the reality that some or many will not immediately buy into your vision?

- Did you complete your research and identify what gaps related to your vision will positively impact the business outcomes of those leaders you need to convert?

- Have you put in the time and made your rounds with key influencers through one-on-one meetings before presenting to an overall audience?

By assessing these factors and steps, you give yourself more clarity and greater opportunity to evolve your power.

Control the Narrative

While new opportunities and promotions fill us all with excitement, for some within diverse groups, these feelings get disrupted by self-defeating thoughts that take up significant headspace. It's like flashing bright neon signs that read:

- Do most people believe I got this promotion or opportunity because of the diversity I represent?

- Am I truly capable of delivering at this new level?

- Can I trust and count on those around me to be vested in my success?

- Will I be able to discern the subtle bias that may come along as a result of this new role and promotion?

These are the wearing thoughts that cause us to worry about being undermined by others. Overcoming these potential roadblocks requires resilience and grit.

During a women's development program that I facilitated, a participant stood up to share her experience: "Nellie, one of my colleagues borderline told me during our conversation that I got promoted simply because I am a woman." Her discomfort and disappointment were visible, and I could see by the expressions of others in the room that this was a familiar scenario. No surprise. Women across industries have dealt with this perception for quite some time. From the podium, I took a few seconds to look around and take in the energy in the room. I wanted other participants to know that I could feel and see their reactions as well.

I responded by posing three important questions. "Do you believe that to be true? Can you control the beliefs and perceptions of others? What power do you have to change that narrative about you?" I explained that, when choosing our response to this type of situation, we must first choose to believe that we have earned this new opportunity or promotion. Second, we must admit that we cannot fully control the beliefs or biases of others. Finally, we must understand that we do have the power to influence our narrative. As such, we do what we have always done: we deliver to our fullest potential and let our results shut down any noise from negative labels or perceptions of others. We give these negative assumptions little to no energy, and instead we align that energy to solving for ourselves, our teams, and the organizations we represent. We have that power.

It was clear that the audience wanted to continue the conversation, and another person asked a follow-up question: "How should we directly respond to those types of comments?"

I gave her a sly smile that hinted at the type of unfiltered reply I sometimes want to give in those moments, but then I gave her my professional response. "Well, let me tell you how I have responded. 'I am looking forward to the value I will add at this new level. I welcome advice, thoughts, ideas, or recommendations you may have for me as I focus on meeting the goals associated with this role.'" Notice that my response did not include phrases like "I am grateful, I am appreciative, or I am so excited about this promotion." That is not by accident. I focused on my value and opened the door to any thoughts or recommendations related to how I could be successful in meeting my goals. I always welcome and acknowledge people's input. I will not, however, feed into commentary that attempts to diminish my accomplishments. When we fail to claim our space and we allow others to minimize us, we may also start to minimize ourselves without even realizing it.

Let's look at some scenarios that display how each of these examples can play out in our professional lives:

Being overly gracious, grateful, and accommodating to others:

- We continuously state how appreciative we are for our positions and opportunities "given to us." It shows up in how we engage in email correspondence when we insert lots of politeness before and after the actual substance of the message. We filter our words through numerous lenses, spending our valuable time reading and rereading our crafted emails before hitting that send button. It can all be quite consuming. Here's an example:
  - *Thank you for the opportunity you have provided me! I appreciate you thinking of me and believing in me! I am so excited about*

having been selected! I am looking forward to showcasing my value. I will not let you down! Please let me know if there is anything I can help you with in the meantime.

I would never suggest not being gracious, grateful, or accommodating. However, I do suggest that we decipher when that behavior is appropriate and sincere, versus when there is a need to be an obliger or make others feel overly appreciated. We need to focus on what we have earned versus what we believe has been gifted to us. Here's what that looks like:

- *I am looking forward to engaging in the new role. Thank you for recognizing my skills and experience and the value both will add. Appreciating your sponsorship.*

Apologizing for our own perspectives:

- I once decided to count the number of times I apologized in a single day. It was 17 times! But I am not alone in this minimizing habit. I often see members of diverse groups apologize for going first or for having to interrupt in order to show up. We even apologize for correcting something or someone, though we know we are right. Think about how often you apologize on any given day. Are those apologies warranted, or do they come from a place of wanting to be accepted or overly accommodating?

- I have seen so many scenarios where people of color find themselves in situations where they have incredibly powerful insights to contribute to conversations. Yet their hyper-awareness of wanting to be perceived in a collaborative and nonthreatening way makes them overly cautious in how they openly share and/or deliver their input, challenge a thought, or disagree. We find ourselves understanding that if we are one of a few or the only in the room, we are tasked with ensuring that our engagement disarms the biases first, so that our input can be welcomed and positively received. This is why many times we will hear people of color starting a sentence, with "I am sorry, but let me . . ." Or "Let me apologize in advance, but . . ." Or "Sorry, can I . . ." This is our heavy burden of constantly accommodating others so that they will embrace us and our input. This goes beyond the politeness culturally instilled in us. This is us adjusting to a corporate environment where we need to find techniques (which feels required only of us) to simply have an opportunity to part take in discussions.

- Instead of using those apologetic intros, I have intentionally shifted to statements like "Adding to what has been said," or "Inserting some thoughts here to . . ." or "Agree with all or most of what has been said; however, let me share another perspective . . ." By shifting to these, I immediately began to feel more accomplished, assertive, and productive.

Giving up opportunities we have earned to others:

- Too often we give up our space, our seat, and our opportunities to others. We do it either in the spirit of "collaboration" or we do it because we simply do not feel ready to be more visible and confidently claim what we have earned. During a conversation with a team member, I shared my decision to evolve her role. Her response was one of polite resistance. She simply did not believe she could take on the expanded scope and even mentioned other people I should consider. I told her, "I am confident in my decision to select you. Why are you trying to convince me otherwise?"

- Unfortunately, the reality is that this scenario plays out too often across various diverse groups. We may opt out because we feel an incredible amount of pressure to convince ourselves we are 100% ready. We are not comfortable with gifting ourselves any room for those critically important learning curves. Other times, we don't believe we truly have the sponsorship required to survive a more demanding and visible role. And then there is the belief and the politeness ingrained in us of not wanting to take an opportunity away from someone else.

• Instead of "Why me?" or "I don't think I am the right choice," or "I don't think I am ready. I need more time," get comfortable with "Thank you, I am looking forward to getting started," "What are the expectations of the role?" and "How do you envision the transition?"

Not boldly promoting ourselves, our skills, or our expertise:

• Immediately after a weekly team call, I reached out to one of the executives on the team to ask her why she wasn't actively engaging on our calls. There was no sugarcoating the question. I was very familiar with her level of expertise, as well as her incredible ability to motivate others, and both had been missing during recent calls. She said, "Nellie, I am being mindful of feedback that has been shared about me that I take up too much space. So I am aiming to tailor that." I was not expecting that response, and we immediately walked through it together. We determined that the feedback was coming from just one colleague and identified some potential reasons why that person would choose to spread that narrative. We then focused on the need for her not to let that feedback completely shut her down. Not only was it harmful for her, but it was also harmful for others who would be stripped of the opportunity to learn from her.

- As members of diverse communities, we need to boldly amplify our voices when opportunities arise, without fear of being perceived as "taking up too much space." I shed that fear midway through my journey as I began recognizing the power of self-promotion. Years before the "elevator pitch" became a branding necessity, I decided to always have a script at the ready for any opportunity to highlight my value to the organization. I invested time in outlining the skills I had attained and rehearsing how I would promote myself to leaders with confidence and ease.

Expecting or accepting limited investment from leaders in our professional development and alignment to opportunities:

- If we are not receiving the level of investment in our upskilling, then we must consider whether we are being too complacent about holding our leadership and organization accountable for their responsibility in providing opportunities for our growth. We should all expect our leadership to invest in us, so ask yourself these questions: Are you being selected to participate in development programs within your organization? If yes, are you investing in yourself to gain the most of those programs, or are you a passive participant? If you are not being selected, do you have clarity as to why not? And will you choose to engage with your leadership to ensure you are selected in the future?

Choosing to take an inactive stance when devalued:

- One person's intentional action and/or storyline about us can lead to a broader narrative about our worth. In some cases, the action is visible and obvious: a leader who refuses to further our professional development or intentionally places hurdles in the way of our advancement. In other cases, seeds are quietly planted, creating a narrative about you that could potentially impact your credibility and derail your success. Choosing not to address it in a balanced and productive manner can negatively influence the course and trajectory of your career. It is important to take charge of these situations. Don't leave these things to chance in hopes that they will go away.

Feeling concerned about being perceived as too ambitious:

- There are times when we have aspirational career goals, but we hesitate to share them with those who can help us reach them, convincing ourselves that we should "wait our turn" instead of being assertive. We worry about being labeled as overly ambitious. There is absolutely nothing wrong with being ambitious. There is everything right about letting leaders and our network know what we aspire to accomplish and demonstrating our abilities to do so. We can't expect leaders to read our minds. Define your ambition strategy. Identify which key leaders may play a part in helping you achieve your goals. Put them on notice.

When you fail to claim your space and allow others to minimize you, you must ask yourself some hard questions. What are the facts and do they align with what you are experiencing? How is the situation impacting you? How long are you willing to accept being devalued by taking a neutral stance and not acting? Can you handle this on your own, or do you need to seek

When you fail to claim your space and allow others to minimize you, you must ask yourself some hard questions.

advice from trusted advisors? At one point in my career, I had to ask myself all these questions. I was in a challenging situation where I needed to address the lack of support from a leader. I took time to seek understanding of the situation and decided to take an active stance in changing it. I needed a balanced approach, so I sought guidance from my trusted advisor and sponsor. It was not an easy step to take, but it was a necessary one. I voiced my concerns with the leader, sharing the impact my leadership's lack of support had on me, and offering potential solutions to resolve the situation. I chose to solve not only for me, but also for the team I was leading and the success of the program as a whole.

The fact that I had already built my credibility and established a strong brand worked in my favor, but even if you are more junior in your career, it is never too early to intentionally select your trusted advisors. It is important to take charge of situations that will impact your career. Make a firm decision to address them in a balanced and productive manner. Even as a junior employee, you can assess your current network and ask yourself some important questions:

- Is your network too insular to your current project, assignment, or team?

- Do you currently have access to supervisors or leaders who clearly have a brand of influence?

- Is there an opportunity to expand your network through Employee Resource Groups?

Once you identify one or two leaders whom you want to get to know, you should seize opportunities by sending an introductory email requesting a quick chat or by introducing yourself at a company event, followed by a brief connection. Be proactive and take the initiative to engage. That is a key piece to evolving your career and ensuring continued mentorship and support.

I recognize that people who are not part of an underrepresented group will say that they too must work through doubts and barriers. I understand that everyone has their own unique journey and experiences. But the disparity is that underrepresented diverse groups face biases that ultimately place more hurdles in our paths. The trepidation we feel in being perceived as too ambitious is an example directly tied to the relentless biases we are already battling. Adding more to that reality positions us to understand that attracting more attention to ourselves, without knowing how it may or may not work against us, is a risk.

Choose Yourself

As the global D&I lead, I found that my responsibility evolved to leading the Accenture Global Women's Program in the early to mid-2000s. When we were planning our upcoming Accenture International Women's Day event, the steering committee was identifying senior women to be part of the event. During one of the planning sessions, I declared that I was going to moderate the mainstage women's executive panel. This was going to be a massive event livestreamed to thousands of people, both internally and externally. Historically, the panel included solely high-profile senior-level women from within the business, with limited HR representation. At the time, I was a senior manager and had not yet reached the leadership ranks. So everyone was surprised when I boldly created my space. I was determined to be a visible part of this event for a few reasons. First, not one Latina had been selected to take part in the broadcast, so I chose to be that representation. Secondly, I saw no reason why a mid-level HR executive could not be a visible part of the day. Most importantly to my journey, I chose to claim my space and gave myself the power in that moment. I took a risk on me.

On the day of the event, I decided to make another statement as well by showcasing the presence and power of a Latina. When I introduced myself as the moderator for the panel, I said, "Hello, hola . . . I am Nellie Borrrrrrrrero!" I let those Rs roll with intensity, pronouncing my last name with my native Spanish tongue. I didn't want to "Anglo" my name on such a big stage. I knew people from all over Latin America would be dialing into the broadcast, and I wanted my "Latinaness" to shine through. I also wanted to send a message to all people across the globe, inside and outside of Accenture, that we should all be proud of our heritage!

Being on that stage with so many amazing women, I knew that I was part of something much bigger than myself. I felt incredibly empowered, and I loved every single thing about that moment. I smiled, took a deep breath, and began to moderate. Instead of sitting next to the panelists, I decided to stand at the podium and assert my presence so as to not fade into the background. As very high-level executives, they were so far removed from me professionally that I felt the need to ensure that the audience experienced us equally. By making that decision, I created a new standard for myself to leverage that position and claim that space in a way that left little room for people's doubts.

The event turned out to be a big success. So many people reached out to comment on my performance, and especially the authentic pronunciation of my last name. Some decisions may seem small, but the impact of my boldness at that moment was received in such a powerful way.

Sometimes, choosing yourself means:

1. Challenging the statement "This is the way it's always been done."
2. Creating innovative and new ideas where you can insert and position yourself to be seen through them
3. Deciding when moments of expected assimilation would be better served by creating awareness of your authenticity and what you represent
4. Positioning yourself by constantly preparing and upskilling to be ready and seize opportunities when they present themselves or when you carve them out
5. Not being a passive observer, and instead being a proactive contributor

My actions that day transcended the event, with people who didn't participate sending me messages about how my one act served as a symbol of acceptance and pride. After that day, I began showing up very differently and I was perceived very differently. And I have pronounced my last name in its authentic Spanish form ever since.

Bet on Your Value

Several years ago, I was sponsoring a leadership program in Europe when I received an email from the COO at the time asking to speak with me. Now, when you get a direct request to call a COO, two opposing thoughts can pop into your head: "Yikes, what did I do?" or "Yay, I can't wait to hear why they want to connect." As I wrapped up the leadership session, I couldn't help but wonder whether this call was going to be a yikes or a yay moment. He started the conversation by asking how the session was going and thanking me for my leadership. Then he said, "Nellie, I now need you to go to South Africa to help us evolve our diversity focus. You are the right person to partner with the local leadership." It was a yay call! How rewarding it was that I had worked myself into a position where I was being directly asked by our COO to engage in something that was important to him and our organization. His words were filled with confidence in my abilities, and they affirmed the importance of my role within the organization. I couldn't wait to embark on this opportunity and have a positive impact in South Africa.

From previous experiences throughout other countries, I knew the drill. I had to research the country, the history, the culture, and the challenges specifically associated with the corporate culture. The weight of this responsibility was not lost on me as a woman, as a Latina, as an American. I put together an entire agenda and flew approximately 15 hours to Johannesburg. I was not only going to focus on the leadership team, but also meet with people across all levels. I wanted to feel and hear from as many people as I could. But I also faced a challenge: I had to work hard to help leaders recognize and appreciate the value I could add to their geography. I expected their hesitation. I could understand how they might question what I could possibly offer. What cultural relevance did I possess that would position me to provide effective insights into solving for local challenges? So it was not a total surprise that the first three days of my visit were quite challenging. Every leader on my agenda canceled our meetings. The woman who was hosting me and my team member,

Carolina, continuously apologized. I could tell that she was incredibly embarrassed. I did not allow these challenges to defeat me, though. Instead, I found ways to fill those now empty time slots by walking around and simply talking to people in the hallways, cafeteria, and even the rest rooms. The conversations were insightful, and I was focusing on one of the things I enjoy the most: human connections. I seized that unplanned available time to be productive in other ways. Once again, I determined to reach my goals.

I had one day left of my visit and was feeling the pressure to ensure that I delivered on the expectations set by the COO. I needed to leave with a plan, a strategy, and proposed actions. I woke up that morning and asked myself, "What am I really good at?" The answers were being courageous and claiming my space. There it was. The reminder I needed. I redirected my thoughts and devised a plan to be consistent with my brand.

I confidently walked into that building on the last day with a much different stride than when I had first arrived, determined to make my way into the office of the managing director. As I breezed by the executive assistant, she quickly called out to me, saying that he was on a call and had no time to meet. I looked back, smiled at her, and said, "No worries. I have time to wait." I walked into his office, pulled up a chair, and sat across from his desk.

He looked at me sternly, but also with a bit of confusion as to why I had just walked into his office unannounced. He wrapped up his call and asked me, "What can I do for you?"

I smiled and said, "The question is more like, what can I do for you if you let me. I am going to get on that plane tonight and fly back 15 hours. I can either use that time to think about how to tell our COO that not one leader would meet with me while I was here, or I can take those 15 hours to work on the strategy that you and I design to help you shine, evolve our diversity focus locally, and simply create greater opportunities for our people." I paused a moment to let my words sink in before continuing: "It's your choice to make right now."

I assumed from the look on his face that no one had ever spoken to him that directly before. Though I usually let those types of awkward silences sit and marinate, I decided to add another flavor to the conversation by saying, "I really like that picture of Colin Powell on your wall. He is such a great human being, isn't he?" He gave a small smile and said, "Let's work on the latter. I have 15 minutes . . . and yes, Colin Powell is an amazing leader."

Before I could filter what I was going to say next, I heard myself say, "No, you are going to give me an hour. That is what I need from you." I still smile every time I recall that moment. That single moment sparked years of amazing partnership and friendship.

I knew from the very beginning that I, together with the local leadership, would make a significant impact in South Africa. But I also knew that I needed to convince them of my ability to add value. I needed to plan, prepare, and demonstrate a collaborative team spirit. If I had given up on that first visit without doing everything I could to be embraced locally, it would have been a tremendous mistake and personal disappointment. There was no doubt in my mind that, given the opportunity to share what I could do for our practice in South Africa, I would be embraced as a leader. Having that clarity and strong belief in myself gave me no other choice but to confidently position myself.

Boosting Your Power

As part of my evolving role, I was excited to expand my landscape and include Latin America as my next focused area to increase our women executive representation. One of my initial stops would be Brazil, but during my first call with local leaders, I met some resistance: "We do not need a program. We have lots of great things happening for our women within our workforce here." I was operating under the awareness that our global leadership had already communicated their commitment to expanding our women executive representation globally. I was keenly aware that I needed to assert myself, engage these leaders, and convince them of the incredible impact that this initiative would have both for women and for the company overall. However, local leadership was curious about how positioning the program would yield results and was concerned about the impact on those who might be feeling excluded from the program. These are fair and expected points and questions, particularly when we are aiming to evolve a culture. It requires budget, leadership backing, and an indication that it will solve for reducing or closing existing gaps and advancing the business.

I partnered with a woman leader in Brazil. She agreed that a focused program would be beneficial to the local culture, which made me even more determined to engage and lead. I knew this would create some discomfort, and I decided to tap into my strength: building relationships. I went to two women leaders in our organization: the CFO, who was very focused on the advancement of women globally, and a female board member who had roots in Brazil. Realizing that I had just upped the game by partnering with these two high-profile women, I was deliberate with my message to Brazil leadership: "I am so pleased to share with you that we're going to have two incredible women come with me to Brazil, our CFO and a board member. Let's quickly work on calendar options in order to confirm dates." Almost instantly, their assistant sent me a message asking to schedule a call.

When we spoke, they were curious about why I was bringing the leaders with me on the trip. My response was, "Globally, our leadership is committed and focused on the advancement of women. As a result, I am partnering with various senior leaders to further this goal." That resulted in a much more positive tone and level of engagement from them. Sometimes we need to engage other leaders to boost our credibility and help us achieve our goals. Tapping into these two women opened the doors more gently and quickly for me to create opportunities that benefited our women and our organization. One of the most valuable lessons I learned from that experience was that sometimes you need to reinforce your power by asking influential and well-established leaders to co-sponsor your initiatives.

We arrived in Brazil to find a buzz around our presence and a lot of positive energy among the women across all levels. Though I sensed reservation among some male leaders, there was also a sense of curiosity. We decided to divide and conquer with two main objectives. The CFO and board member spent time with one of the most senior leaders talking through the business case for our women development initiative, while my role was to bring the voices of women across all levels of the organization to life to highlight existing challenges. There was a lot of engagement in those conversations, but once the CFO and board member departed, I was left to deal with some of the original resistance to the program from a very few.

At the start of the first inclusion training program, I got up to introduce myself to the group of leaders and share the objectives of the session. Many of the participants were familiar to me because I had already met with them throughout the week. After I finished my introduction, one of the leaders who had originally challenged me the most also addressed the group. He decided to speak in Portuguese, which I didn't speak. Though I didn't know what he was saying at the time, I could clearly see and feel the level of discomfort in the room. After a few minutes, I asked the woman sitting next to me what was going on. Why was everyone speaking in Portuguese? She informed me that the leader wanted the course to be taught in Portuguese, even though everyone in the room was fluent in English. His actions bothered me because I knew he would not have done that had the CFO and board member still been present. However, I didn't show my discomfort. Instead, I let the training continue because I knew I would be able to turn it around given the right moment.

That moment came when someone asked a question to the broader group, and I saw several of the participants look my way. I quickly stood up and said, "Excuse me. I don't fully understand the question you asked since I don't understand Portuguese, but I would imagine that I could probably help answer based on my expertise and experience, which is why I am here." The participant gladly rephrased the question in English, and we had a very good dialogue, with others joining in. As we wrapped up that exchange, I could see the displeasure of the leader who had instructed everyone to speak in Portuguese. In response, I said, "I do understand that our CFO and our board member are no longer here, but I'm here." It was a stern statement, but one that was necessary to proclaim my leadership status and power. I chose to focus my energy where it needed to be, which was on the participants in the room.

Ensuring that women or any demographic that is underrepresented have equal pathways to succeed requires leadership to lead with the mindset that diversity is an accelerator that positively impacts organizational results. These two factual points must be ingrained into every diversity-related conversation:

1. Diverse talent creates a business advantage in the ever-present multicultural and global marketplace.
2. Diversity undoubtedly spurs innovation, increasing access to new customers, partnership, and/or clients.

Simply put, diversity provides organizations with a business edge and advantage.

We ended up executing an amazing and successful women's program in Brazil as the leadership team became increasingly engaged and supportive in evolving the culture. We know that change is not easy for everyone. But my experience has shown me that those who are not willing to adapt eventually see others move on and evolve while they stay behind, ultimately halting their own professional growth. Change agents are required, and I have always welcomed the opportunity to take on that role.

Know Your Worth

There are so many reasons why it is significantly important for us to pause and define our own professional worth. Our understanding of our worth evolves and increases as we continue to build on our skills and gain further experiences. But we must first unapologetically and continuously claim, embrace, and verbalize our own worth before we hope or expect others to recognize and respect it. We do this by maintaining an awareness about the internal dialogue we ourselves are permitting and fueling. We become disciplined and intentional about always being prepared and delivering our best. Yes, systemic biases exist. But we can combat them by choosing to create and nurture our circle of trusted advisors throughout our careers, courageously speaking up to advocate for ourselves and designing our paths towards greater opportunities.

Throughout my career, I have been keenly aware of the worth I possess. That doesn't mean that I haven't had doubts along the way. But even when those doubts penetrated my space, my strong awareness of my worth fueled my ability to conquer them. While I have always understood the importance of empowering myself to claim my space, I also acknowledge how the energy infused in me by leaders, colleagues, and teammates played a role in creating an environment where I could navigate my success.

As I close this chapter, I want to share an amazing experience. While at home on a Saturday morning, I began to receive multiple text messages in succession from my Hispanic American/Latinx professional network. One was from Cid Wilson, President and CEO of the Hispanic Association on Corporate Responsibility (HACR). It read, "Julie Sweet spoke great about you at the L'ATTITUDE Conference. She referred to you as her mentor. Congratulations Nellie on being a 5-time Most Powerful Latina and for being inducted into the inaugural Hall of Fame."

Now, let me break this down. Three major things were happening here. First, I was being inducted into the Association of Latino Professionals for America's (ALPFA) Hall of Fame, which was quite an accomplishment. Second, this recognition was being announced at the L'ATTITUDE Conference, which focuses on evolving the Hispanic American/Latinx community and tapping into its economic power. Third, Accenture CEO Julie Sweet, who is a highly regarded global leader with incredible accolades, including Forbes #1 CEO, mentioned my name in her speech. Though having Julie publicly share how she views our professional relationship is incredibly rewarding, I don't typically pause to experience and absorb moments like these. But I gave myself the space to absorb the meaning of the moment—I had reached milestones that my younger self couldn't even imagine.

As you are going through your own experiences of questioning your power, take a moment to pause, courageously assess what is happening, and make choices that push you to solve for yourself and believe in your power.

Questions for Consideration

1. How are you recognizing and showcasing your worth?

2. How can you help empower yourself and other underrepresented professionals?

3. What are some ways you can challenge the status quo and show up for yourself authentically?

Choosing to Lead with an Inclusive Mindset

"Nellie, I am trying to mentor a person of color, but I don't sense a great amount of interest or excitement in return." This is a sentiment I often hear from executives who choose to mentor employees of color. Their perception does not surprise me. Many see mentoring as a way of doing their part in solving for equity and equality and helping their mentees reach new heights. They go into it with excitement, a lot of energy, and high hopes for the immediate impact they can make. So when those initial expectations go unmet, they may feel personally rejected or believe that their time is not being valued.

Then there is the other side of the relationship. As a person of color in a corporate environment, the mentee may feel guarded and hesitant about immediately divulging all aspects of their professional experiences or aspirations, no matter how essential communication is for building a mentor/mentee relationship. Two crucial questions typically come up for people of color when faced with this situation: Should I feel comfortable sharing? Can I trust this person? The answers to these questions influence our initial engagement—engagement that may be perceived as lack of interest or excitement by the mentor.

Many people of color were raised not to immediately trust people outside of our culture. We consciously or unconsciously adhere to the warning instilled in us to "proceed with caution." So when someone attempts to penetrate that very well-protected and private space, we default to these lessons and ask ourselves questions like: Why is this person interested in me? Am I simply a "diversity" checklist action item for them? We are also discerning some of our own lived experiences within our corporate environments, prompting reminders of microaggressions, isolation, and/or marginalization. Each of these concerns chips away at our ability to feel fully confident or trusting of their intentions.

These initial reactions make it challenging to experience an immediately natural and fluid connection, even though they often take place in conjunction with a strong inclination to receive mentoring and build it into our career development. As you can see, there is much to solve for. A successful mentoring relationship requires mutual consideration, energy, and effort, all anchored on trust.

During a conversation I had with an Afro Latino employee, he mentioned being selected to participate in a formal mentoring program. He wondered about the selection process. Had the mentor selected him, or had someone else made the match? This is the type of curiosity that a mentee experiences when chosen for these types of programs. The mentor showed up for the first meeting very enthusiastic, confidently detailing all the ways the organization needed to increase its diversity and his commitment to this goal. However, the mentee had some apprehension. Boom! An immediate disconnect. While both were eager to get started, the mentee was looking for confirmation that the mentor was the right match and was vested in him personally, while the mentor was looking to demonstrate his commitment to solving for diversity gaps. Each arrived with positive intentions, in the lane that they felt was important to the mentoring relationship. But the mentee was left with a bit of skepticism about the mentor's genuine interest in him as an individual.

When a person decides to invest in somebody and unlock opportunities for them, they should always start from a transparent human connection. They should ask themselves: What are our similarities and common interests? How do I leverage those for initial connections? What are our clear differences? How do we acknowledge those? What actions do I need to take to demonstrate my genuine interest in engaging? When they fail to sort through these vital questions and steps, it elongates the path to fruitful connections.

Access Granted, But Not Ready

One evening, on a typical night at home, I was sitting across from my daughter, who was a teenager at the time. She sat on the couch with her legs crossed, engaged in the scarf that she was crocheting, while I was just about to turn in for the night. Something weighed on my mind that evening, though, and my fashionable daughter seemed like the perfect person to help. Before getting up to leave the room, out of the blue I asked her, "Ginaly, what designer pajamas do you think corporate women executives wear? I need you to help me select one."

Her reaction was comical. She whipped her head around so fast that she inadvertently dropped the crochet needle. The look on her face was both impatient and inquisitive as she leaned forward in a very exaggerated way and said, "Umm, why in the world are you asking that?" I shared with her that Pamela Craig, the CFO of Accenture, had invited her local mentee network to her beautiful summer home for dinner and a sleepover, followed by a morning walk on the beach. It sounded amazing and I felt privileged to have been included. However, while excited by the invitation, I also felt some slight anxiety. This event would be hours and hours of engagement. I wondered if I would be able to fit in, or how much would I need to push myself out of my comfort zone to simply relax and enjoy the experience. As I sat in my family room that evening, I envisioned all of us chilling in our pajamas, casually chatting and having a cup of tea at Pam's house. It quickly dawned on me that these incredibly successful women would probably wear pajamas that were as fashionable as their work attire. I decided it was time to up my pajama game or, as my daughter eventually schooled me, my loungewear. Ultimately, new loungewear was purchased, but that did not remove my anxieties.

I've had many mentors throughout my journey. Each has served a different purpose, and several have been key influences in my career, but Pam has been one of the most influential. She has been an incredible ally and someone I consider a friend. Yet our journey went through many cycles, some of which she still is not aware. Her stature seemed so incredibly high, intimidating, and unreachable to me. My initial resistance to our relationship had nothing to do with her as a person. Instead, it reflected my own experiences and beliefs. I had placed her on a pedestal, and I had to work through the doubts that lingered in my head about my ability to comfortably engage with someone at that level. Without fail, each meeting with her was preceded by my asking myself an entire list of questions. What am I going to talk about? How prepared am I for the meeting? What am I going to wear? How do I showcase my appreciation for her mentorship? How do I make this worthy of her time as well? How do I respond to her requests in a way that showcases my capabilities?

> *When . . . you are the only diverse one, or part of a very few represented in that room, your inner voice begins to point out and highlight your differences.*

My relationship with Pam began around a common interest. At a junior point in my career, I saw her speak on a panel, and I latched on to her every word. She spoke with such impressive ease as she unapologetically asserted the need to do more for the advancement of women at the leadership level. Because I was in the diversity space, I saw her as a critically important advocate and ally, with a common interest in the women's agenda. I was inspired to channel her assertiveness, so I proactively scheduled time on her calendar. Initially, I viewed our relationship as a singularly focused connection driven by a common goal. However, once we connected, I realized that Pam viewed our relationship with a broader stroke. She made a choice to expand our engagement and play a more influential role in my career, which included pulling me into the circle of women whom she mentored. The reality of being exposed at that level initially intimidated me, and I felt an immediate need to put up a wall. I was out of my comfort zone, and I couldn't figure out how to show up with Pam in a way that I could feel fully at ease. I didn't have access to some of the very well-crafted mentoring models and road maps that exist today, including ways to design a plan for the relationship, top questions to ask, and advice for sharing mutual expected outcomes. I had to figure it out on my own. What I did have was my understanding that we shared a very important and mutual common goal in solving for increased diversity. I also had my cultural superpowers—relationships: how to establish them and how to nurture them!

A dynamic takes place when you are selectively included. It could occur through a team, someone's networking circle, a project, a conference, a business dinner . . . or a mentorship. When these opportunities present themselves and you are the only diverse one, or part of a very few represented in that room, your inner voice begins to point out and highlight your differences. Being included in Pam's circle with her invitation to the sleepover forced me to engage with many other incredible senior-level women. I was aware of my differences. "I am the only one here with my lived experiences and cultural references. How do I show up in a confident way without feeling worn down in the process?" Within the corporate environment, we as women of color do not have the liberty that other people have to show up authentically without fear of judgment or backlash. The thoughts were like a filter, causing me to be very guarded about every conversation.

I don't know if any of the other women felt the same pressure, but for many people of color, it is a reality that we cannot ignore. We ruminate on the realities of our differences and the multiple ways by which we need to protect ourselves emotionally. I once heard someone say that when you are the only one or one of a few in a room, it can feel like there is an asterisk beside your name. I felt the weight of that asterisk as I tried to prepare myself for the sleepover, but I also knew that I had to reject my own filters of doubt in order to truly experience a level of comfort. When conversations took place that were not relatable to me and my lived experiences, I had to redirect my thoughts away from feelings of inferiority. International vacations, second or third homes, private schools, and personal trainers—none of that was part of my world at the time. I knew it was completely unintentional on the part of the other women, but these conversations reminded me of the gaps that existed in our lived experiences, ultimately making me feel excluded while included. I could have used those feelings as an excuse to shrink inward and not engage, but I chose to take responsibility for my own thoughts instead. I refused to give that negativity any damaging or diminishing energy, mindfully choosing to embrace the opportunity I had been granted and leveraging it to evolve. Pam had invited me in. I had to choose to partake.

In hindsight, I truly enjoyed that first sleepover at Pam's house, and I was so glad that I went. Receiving that invitation had created such apprehension on my part that I was hoping for any excuse not to attend, even going as far as envisioning myself in a fender bender that would stop me from getting to her house. It took me getting out of my own way before I could simply allow myself to enjoy and be present in the moment.

Pam had created something very powerful, which at the time I had not fully realized. She brought together women across various levels. By opening her home and hosting casual events for us, she gave us access to one another, and created a space for bonding that transcended into our working relationships. There were many more dinners and sleepovers at Pam's. The relationships that I forged through those invitations unlocked many amazing opportunities. I became less hesitant when other leaders attempted to connect with me and began to feel more comfortable through the experiences I was embracing. Pam and I went on to travel the world together, prioritizing the women's agenda. We evolved the women of color scope and led several inaugural women's leadership programs, inclusive of an amazing experience in Japan. Many senior women leaders engaged in sponsoring our global women's agenda. Initially, I resisted Pam's mentorship, but I am grateful that she persisted, leading to an incredible relationship.

Mentoring: An Investment and a Reward

I have mentored people all around the world, and one thing has been consistent: they have gotten the most out of the relationship when I courageously engaged in necessary yet challenging conversations for them to grow and reach their goals.

One of my long-time mentees recently reached out to request some time with me. As we jumped on a video call, her usual wide smile and cheerful self had been replaced with a palpable concerning expression. "Nellie, I believe that I have put myself in a position where I may have caused my leadership to question my abilities. I have been thinking about this and I am convinced that there may be no way for me to redeem myself because my inability to effectively deliver was very visible to our top leadership." During a high-stakes, pressure-driven discussion with the most senior C-level business leaders, my mentee had been unable to demonstrate her expertise and get the leaders to reach the desired outcome, and she felt rattled and defeated.

I have always told my mentees to call me if they ever find themselves questioning their value to the organization and whether they belong there. There are two reasons for this. First, I advise them never to accept a new job in order to run away from something. Rather, they should run *to* something that is worth it and has been well thought out. Second, I want to have a conversation about how I can help them stay. Following my advice to call me, my mentee talked about her thought process and her belief that her career had hit a bump too difficult to overcome. She shared her plan to lay low for a while and simply do her work while in the process of actively seeking external opportunities.

I listened without interrupting, giving her the opportunity to tell her full story, but also to have her hear herself out loud. Once she was done, I said, "Thank you for sharing this. I am sorry you have had this experience, and I know how bad you feel. I've known you for over a decade and I know this experience does not define you or all you have accomplished." I went into mentor mode with the goal of helping her see her way out of the situation.

I needed to be nurturing but assertive, while fearlessly probing with questions that would lead her to the right decision. I saw her value and wanted her to see it for herself, too. I didn't want her to give up and leave. It was not the right answer for her or the organization.

I began with these questions:

- How hard have you worked to reach your level?
- How disappointed and upset at yourself are you going to be if you choose to be silent without speaking up for yourself?
- Would you coach other women not to advocate for themselves under similar circumstances?
- Why would you choose not to courageously course-correct what went wrong?
- What are the potential lessons to gain from this experience?
- Why wouldn't you share those learned lessons with your leadership?
- Why would you choose to run away?

I could see her discomfort with all of my questions, but her smile eventually worked its way back. "Nellie, this is hard and exhausting, but your questions are spot on."

I smiled and responded, "Since when have you ever taken the easy path? Don't start now because you made such a visible mistake." We continued our conversation, and she ultimately reached the conclusion that advocating for herself was the only answer that she could ultimately feel good about. She recognized that not doing so would strip away pieces of the brand she had built for herself.

Most of us encounter some moments where we feel we have made a career-limiting mistake. It feels terrible, and our first reaction may be to tell ourselves it is time to test the job market and consider leaving. Mentoring relationships should reach a level where the mentees can be transparent with how they are feeling, and even vulnerable in some cases. They should reach a point where the mentor can challenge the mentee's thoughts or decisions if they are clearly misaligned with whom they have shaped themselves to be. Mentor roles are meant to walk mentees through not only the pleasant and easy conversations but also the difficult ones where they are being prompted to see the full picture, including the impact of their thoughts and actions. Sometimes we are quick to judge. But if we operate with the mindset of judging less and mentoring more, we can have an incredible influence in bringing out the magic each person has to offer.

There are two ever-present questions when organizations think through mentoring:

1. Should mentors be of the same or similar backgrounds of the mentee?
2. In what ways are organic mentorship relationships more effective than prescribed pairings through designed programs?

As at many organizations, we at Accenture also believe that mentoring provides our people with the necessary tools and resources to enhance their performance, achieve their goals, and grow within the organization. As we consider approaches to providing diverse individuals access to mentors, we recognize that mentors and mentees may have immediately stronger connections when they share relatable experiences. However, we also recognize that strong mentoring pairings can also be formed without having those relatable experiences. Ultimately, when mentors focus on further developing talent, providing greater reach, tapping into empowerment, and addressing gaps, they motivate mentees to reach their full potential.

Become the Best Ally You Can Be

Advocating for others has always come natural for me, which is why leading Inclusion & Diversity for over three decades was the perfect path for my career. As a diversity practitioner, I have always understood the responsibility of advocating across underrepresented groups. Very early on, I also recognized the critical role I played as an ally to others. I needed to strategically advocate for change by being an effective and courageous ally. We know that mentorship and sponsorship are critically important resources in one's career, and I believe advocating and allyship should receive just as much emphasis. They are both essential to the creation of a broader culture of inclusion and working towards achieving equality.

Many people ask, "How can I become an effective ally?" I love this question because it signals a genuine desire to really make a difference, not just wear the ally badge for personal gain. There is no single piece of advice that I can offer since we each arrive at this space from different starting points. But there are some internal conversations that we can have to best prepare ourselves and deal with some misguided beliefs that can potentially hinder the allyship.

Misguided Belief #1: "I don't believe in the need for official allies. Each person should be expected to simply behave in a way that supports all." This thinking is not realistic. While I understand the sentiment behind this comment, the unfortunate reality is that not all people behave in a way that supports everyone. We all need allies. In acknowledging that you must understand how and why people and communities benefit from allies, including why it is necessary to the evolution of corporate culture. Allies create entryways and serve as conduits for cultural change benefiting those who have been historically disadvantaged. They are a key component to solving for equality through their role in advocating for inclusion. Many times, they are the voice for those who know it's too risky to advocate for themselves. They can drive change through their roles and networks. Think about the reasons why you want to personally become an ally and identify the driving force behind your decision.

Misguided Belief #2: "I cannot be a good ally for communities that I don't understand or don't have relatable lived experiences." This is totally false. Educating yourself in those differences can be of great value, if you do it with intention. Select the community or communities you are choosing to serve as an ally for and educate yourself about the challenges historically experienced within the community. Today, we have significant clarity related to groups who experience social injustices or biases that carry over into the workplace. There is no mystery about which groups are the most impacted across multiple countries. So how do we educate ourselves? Simple. Dig into media, articles, books, and reports. Seek out members of the impacted communities for greater understanding. Conversations are powerful; staying uninformed is unfortunate.

Also, become familiar with the most pressing challenges existing today. Then think about how you see yourself engaging. Realistically identify the level of time you can commit to being an ally and identify ways to infuse allyship throughout your broader role and level of responsibilities.

Misguided Belief #3: "I am just one person. I will not be able to make a significant impact." Yes, you can. The impact of one person ripples through thousands. Identify the level of impact you wish to have on the community. Consider whether that impact is the best way to serve the community and ask yourself what steps you should take to ensure it.

Being an ally also requires you to become a continuous learner. This is critically important for navigating the missteps that may occur as you evolve through the allyship. We can go into this role with nothing but positive thoughts and still say or do something that contradicts those good intentions. We may mistakenly make an incorrect assumption or not use the proper terminology. We may be at a loss about what to immediately say or how to help in a moment of crisis for the community. These circumstances can make us feel like awkward allies in the moment, but we cannot let that keep us from the larger goal. Sometimes you simply have to acknowledge that you have made a mistake or just didn't know how to help. You have to be willing to partner with the community and people within it to learn and grow. By leveraging your network, power, and influence, you have the ability to meaningfully engage.

As a heterosexual woman and a person of color, I have had a good sense of what type of allyship is required within these communities. And, while I did not have the lived experiences of individuals with a different sexual orientation or identity to mine, I did have a strong desire to solve for the community. I understood early on that we should have an environment where everyone can feel free to show up as who they are. I also knew that I wanted to move on from this narrative of "tolerating" the community to embracing and celebrating it instead! I once heard someone say, "As humans we want to be accepted in five important settings: our family, our community, our religious institutions, our schools, and our workplace." I would also add our circle of friends to that list. I sat with that thought for a while, as I asked myself what power I possess to help the community feel a sense of overall acceptance and inclusion. Where did my power and influence lie? While I could not control the beliefs of an individual's family, religious institution, school, community, or friends, I could have an impact on how to further evolve my workplace culture. That awareness propelled me to advocate for the community at a time when most organizations were not welcoming this movement.

In the mid-'90s, I decided that it was time to move our diversity focus beyond women and ethnic minorities. At the time, we did not yet reference the community as LGBTQI+. We instead used the term "gay community" almost in the form of a whisper. Even the word "lesbian" was barely used within the corporate environment. The comfort level and full understanding of the community simply was not there yet, and I set out on a path to change this with the same level of intensity and strategic focus as I did with other diversity segments. This is when I discovered the intersectionality of diverse segments while also recognizing the uniqueness of each. As I focused on this community, there were enlightening moments and significant learning curves. Each milestone brought about opportunities to evolve our support for the community.

Step 1: Seek Leadership Support

I decided to go to the top and requested to meet with our CEO at the time to discuss the status of our diversity efforts. I felt comfortable doing so because we had traveled together on a visit to Florida A&M University, one of our targeted Historically

Black Colleges and Universities (HBCUs), and I could leverage the familiarity built on that trip. He graciously accepted the meeting, which I concluded with a declaration that it was time to move beyond women and ethnic minorities. "I want to expand our program to include the gay community." Silence. I waited for his response. I could see he was contemplating my words, as he turned away from me and looked out the window. Instead of interrupting his thoughts, I turned to stare in the same direction. He then looked down at his desk. I followed suit and looked down at his desk as well. The silence felt like an eternity. But in that moment, I learned the power of sitting in an uncomfortable situation, not breaking the silence and allowing the other person to work through their thought process.

I was finally able to exhale when I heard him say, "Nellie, are you trying to tell me that you are lesbian?" The question surprised me, but I immediately felt that it was coming from a place of concern. If I was, I sensed that he wanted to understand how to best support me. I responded, "No. I am trying to ensure we are supportive of this community, and we can be one of the first companies to step up and advocate for change." We continued with a dialogue full of many questions.

Two weeks later, he reached out to me and said, "Nellie, go ahead and include this as part of our Diversity Program." My ally and advocate role had achieved a great first step.

Many times it is challenging to get access to leaders, or it may feel intimidating to reach out. I was junior in my career when I did. But I understood what was driving me—the need for cultural change. As you think about reaching out to leaders, ask yourself what is driving you. Why is it important to you? How will it benefit you and the organization? Once you have that clarity, you will feel the internal push to move forward, knowing what or who you are solving for. Have your story line and pitch ready. Reach out, ask for time, and be driven by your intent.

Step 2: Tap into the Community

In my excitement to hurry up and get started, I made one huge first mistake. I reached out to a colleague and asked him for a meeting without warning him what it was about. As he walked into my office, I greeted him with a huge smile. He smiled back and said, "What's up, Nellie?"

I very enthusiastically said, "I have good news! I have support to expand our Diversity Program to include the gay community. I would really appreciate your help in understanding what the community needs and how best to prioritize our programmatic approach." I could feel my breathing getting a bit heavier from my excitement. He, on the other hand, looked at me perplexed. After a few seconds he said, "Sounds great, Nellie. But why are you asking me for help?" Before thinking through my response, I said, "Because you know the community better than I do." OMG! It quickly became obvious that I had dug a hole for myself by acting on someone else's interpretation of his identity or that he would be open to talking about it. I tried to recover by asking if he knew anyone more familiar with the community to help me. But I truly felt terrible.

Several days later, he walked back into my office and closed the door behind him. I was prepared to accept whatever he wanted to dish out at me, but instead, he said, "Nellie, I am not fully out, only to a select few people. Your request took me off guard, but also reminded me of the changes we need to make for people within the community to feel embraced, safe, and accepted." In the years to follow, he ended up being an outspoken and effective leader championing the community.

There were so many incredible people I tapped into, including Richard Clark, who was already on the path to being outspoken. He was fearless and strategic about our internal goals and partnership with external organizations. Our collective strategies sparked a beginning for the relentless path we would embark on to be a corporate global leader.

Seeking out members of communities to help lead efforts is always a good approach. Making assumptions through our own or others' lenses is not. Another reality to be aware of is that, even if you factually know a person is a representative of a community or demographic, that does not translate to their willingness or desire to be an active or visible participant in evolving the community or demographic they represent. Everyone has their own journey and comfort level about whether or not they want to be a spokesperson.

Step 3: Learn and Act

I had a lot to learn about the gay and lesbian community and other communities outside of my lived experiences. Luckily for me, many people within the community were willing not only to call me out when necessary, but also to teach me.

I was on the agenda to speak at a large leadership meeting. It was my first time speaking on the topic of the gay and lesbian community, and I proudly stood on the stage and talked through a slide reflecting our evolving diversity priorities. On the slide, in a very pronounced color and font, I listed the term "Sexual Preference." I wanted it to boldly stand out that we were now including this as a focus area. I then went onto to say the term several times, highlighting our proposed approach. At the time, that was a common phrase used in the few corporate discussions about the "gay community." I exited the stage feeling so accomplished, with no clue of the important lesson I was about to learn.

I could see one of the participants rushing towards me from the corner of my eye. He said, "Nellie, thank you for including the gay community as part of our diversity focus, but for us the term 'sexual preference' is offensive." Ouch! I felt a gut punch. He continued, "It is a reference we need to get rid of. It is our 'sexual orientation.' We do not choose or prefer to be gay."

I gave him a hug and said, "Thank you for educating me. If you had not done so, I would have continued making this mistake over and over. I promise you I will correct every single person whom I hear use that term from now on." And that is exactly what I did. I never missed an opportunity to either privately or publicly correct someone whenever the opportunity arose. I understood that a big part of our responsibility as advocates and allies is to share what we have learned.

I am proud of our ongoing stance within Accenture to support, embrace, and celebrate the LGBTQI+ community. We continue to evolve with the community globally, recognizing that there are multiple facets and complexities that we need to focus on country by country. Throughout my journey as an ally, I have kept learning and growing as we have evolved to represent the broader community encompassing LGBTQI+. As the community has evolved to solve for its people and create a greater sense of inclusion, so has the need to be better informed. Allies have multiple channels by which to educate ourselves, including developing relationships with members of the community. We sometimes hesitate in fear that we will offend with our questions.

There are simple yet impactful ways by which we can make a significant difference for the LGBTQI+ community. For instance, we can be more inclusive in our language by saying, "Good morning, all" or "Hi, everyone" instead of "Ladies and gentlemen." Instead of "You guys," we can say, "You all" or "Any of you." We can replace "Do you have a girlfriend/husband?" with "Do you have a partner?" We can also avoid making assumptions about someone's pronouns by simply sharing our pronouns first or asking, "Can I confirm your pronouns, please?" These small but powerful changes help us to become better allies as we work to craft an environment that is truly safe and inclusive for us all.

In addition to learning, we need to act! Organizations must align funding and resources must also evolve as we solve for the community, including support for external organizations focused on the protection and advancement of the LGBTQI+. In the mid-2000s, one of our focus areas was educating allies, helping them understand the biases and threats towards the community, and how they can use their voices to support. Today this initiative is known as our L3 (LGBTQI+, Leaders, Learning) program. We evolved from simply having allies wear lanyards early on to further educating them in solving for concrete cultural changes that create a more inclusive and embracing environment.

During one of the global L3 presentations, I said, "If you are comfortable, please raise your hand if you are attending this program as an ally." So many hands proudly went up in the air.

I followed with, "That's great. Thank you for being an ally. Now how many are willing to stand up and share one or two actions you have taken in the last couple of months to advocate for the community?" Only two people stood up. I asked this question to drive the important point that acting must be part of allyship. Sometimes our allyship is subtle and other times it is visible, but either format can be impactful. The probing question generated a lot of conversation.

There are various ways, either subtle or visible, that allyship can show up. An ally can be any of the following:

- An Awkward Ally wants to help someone or a group but they don't want to make a misstep by saying or doing the wrong thing and inadvertently offending instead of helping.

- A Courageous Ally will instantly and publicly interrupt and address a bias. They will stop someone from continuing with any type of offensive language, joke, or behavior.

- An Informed Ally seeks to learn as much as they can about the challenges facing those within the community or communities they are advocating for. They are self-aware and understand how much more they need to learn.

- An Outspoken Ally is committed to effecting change within the culture by challenging practices and policies that negatively impact the community or communities they are advocating for. They leverage their voice in prioritizing the focus and commitment required in order to ensure resources and call for accountability to enact change.

- A Passive Ally, while not as outwardly active or outspoken, remains an important ally to the community. Their subtle representation of support may encourage others to become allies and showcase a welcoming space for the community.

Step 4: Keep It Front and Center

As an ally, I have understood that progress does not mean you can claim the small victories and move on. Victories can continue to be challenged, creating a possibility for the reversal and diminishing of progress to date. For this reason, our allyship continues to be essential to an inclusive culture. But it also means that we must continue identifying ways to evolve organizational support to address existing and new challenges.

Our program went global thanks to our C-suite leadership and many leaders who subsequently took on the global sponsorship for this community. We all led with the awareness of creating an environment of acceptance and inclusion, while we were also aware of the huge responsibility to keep members of the LGBTQI+ community safe, particularly in challenging countries. Each time I visited a country, I aimed to include the LGBTQI+ focus to support and connect with the community. During one of my visits to Singapore, I met with members of the community to discuss progress to date, existing country-specific challenges, and our internal goals. One of the members brought a beautiful cake into the conference room and asked me to slice it. It was a rainbow cake, representing the diversity of the community. I quickly sliced up the entire cake. I then proceeded to take slices of it to people's offices, introducing myself and sharing the meaning of the cake. I had so many wonderful and insightful conversations during each of those impromptu meetings, while also eating a whole lot of delicious cake. But the power of that day was beautiful. It was an example of true allyship. Find your window, find that opportunity, leverage it, and keep that conversation moving!

A Culture of Belonging

At Accenture, we want our people to operate from a place of being "Truly Human," which is always a work in progress. When I first heard the term, I wanted to examine how I was showing up as a truly human leader. Did that mean being nice, polite, and nurturing all of the time? For me, engaging in a truly human way has meant respectfully disrupting when required to evoke necessary change and evolve the culture. It also means that our people should feel seen, heard, safe, and courageous. It has meant seeking to understand how to lead with a constant inclusive mindset. Mentoring, advocating, and allyship all lead to our people feeling the support necessary to experience a truly human environment and a culture of belonging.

Questions for Consideration

1. How are you openly embracing opportunities to be mentored?
2. What type of ally are you: Awkward, Courageous, Informed, Outspoken, or Passive?
3. How can your mentoring role be expanded to share your network, position your mentee for opportunities, and recognize unique diversity-related challenges?

CHAPTER

5

The Push-Pull of Personal and Professional Demands

Life happens, and in many cases we are required to accept the setbacks and continuously step forward while acknowledging unwelcome pauses. No matter how hard we try to keep them separate, the challenges of our personal lives often permeate into our work lives. I keep the heaviness in my life in a tight vault where only a very select few have access. Within my culture, there is a fear about being perceived as weak. Showing any weakness is believed to open the door for others to seize those moments and position us at a disadvantage. For communities of color, there is no room for error, so we often keep that vault shut and move forward without the help we otherwise benefit from.

I always planned and positioned myself for the milestones I aspired to achieve. But in that planning, I did not include or foresee divorce, single parenting, illness, or the loss of a loved one as events that would abruptly halt my pace throughout my journey. I also never planned for the impact and disruption that a global pandemic brings. I did not include the level of emotional energy it takes to fully show up professionally, when personally there is internal turmoil and pain.

For me, the lessons I learned along the way have been invaluable. We each handle our challenges differently, but I have found a familiarity when talking to women of color. We constantly put forth this façade of strength even when feeling turmoil inside. We pressure ourselves to keep pushing through to meet our goals with persistence, and even relentless stubbornness. No matter what is thrown our way, we push forward to achieve our professional goals, live out our dreams and those of our ancestors, while providing for our loved ones. But what I have learned over the years is that I have to let go of those pressures I place on myself. We cannot keep showing up while ignoring the effects of

113

these pressures, without regard for our well-being and its impact on our mental health.

My New, Negatively Perceived Label: Divorced, Single Working Mom

Divorce is rarely easy. It brings about a sense of loss and mourning, sometimes accompanied by guilt and even doubt. I felt all of these emotions as I dissolved a 12-year marriage. Though we had both checked out a couple of years prior, I was forced to acknowledge the failure of what was supposed to be a lifelong partnership. Two good people needed to embark on different paths.

It was a difficult realization, but even in the midst of my pain, I was intent on prioritizing the well-being of my nine-year-old daughter, Ginaly. I would be her main caregiver and provider, so having a successful career became more important than ever before. I felt a lot of heaviness from that change in my life. I had become part of a statistic that I never dreamed of being part of. I was navigating unfamiliar and intense emotions, while feeling the incredible need to succeed professionally. I placed a lot of pressure on myself to make up for what I believed my decision had taken away from my daughter, a traditional family unit and all of the perceived security that comes along with that. There was the new challenge of solving for childcare while juggling a calendar filled with work travel, early morning meetings, and evening work-related commitments, not to mention the financial impact of handling everything on my own. It became a nagging and unyielding internal conversation that noisily took up a lot of my headspace, leaving me exhausted and emotionally drained.

When faced with this type of disruptive life event, we need to remind ourselves and others that our new circumstances do not mean that we are less ambitious or less committed to our careers. In fact, our professional aspirations may be even more amplified given our new circumstances and responsibilities. However, the reality of the situation is that, while we can absolutely still reach our goals, the timing may need to be adjusted. Our flexibility and availability may temporarily be impacted, moments may come when we find ourselves saying no to opportunities or events we would've ordinarily jumped at without hesitation. Those moments can feel awful, especially if we dwell on the feeling of missing out. But those are the moments when we are responsibly managing the priorities of our new reality. Navigating change successfully may require difficult conversations with leadership about our changing circumstances and our plans to solve for them.

Despite spending an entire year preparing myself financially, emotionally, and physically for this new chapter in my life, it was still a very painful transition. The first of anything on my own triggered sadness. Birthdays, holidays, and even the oil change warning light in my car left me in tears. I was also extremely vulnerable during that time. I was constantly stressed, which did not go unnoticed by a leader at the time.

Sitting across from him at a nearby restaurant, I finally revealed that I was going through a separation and did not want anyone at the office to know. We shared an ongoing commitment to increasing diversity. We had established a mutual relatability and supportive professional relationship that allowed me to be vulnerable and confide in him as a trusted advisor, even about this personal challenge.

He asked, "Why don't you want anybody to know?"

I explained to him that I saw myself as a statistic. Another woman of color whose marriage failed. Another woman of color who would become a single parent. I didn't want people to know that something in my life had failed because I feared that it would surface doubts about my ability to deliver. After patiently listening to my explanation, he assured me that I had plenty of colleagues who would be willing to assist me through this rough patch, if I was only willing to ask for help. But I had been afraid of leaders voicing opinions such as, "You know, she is going through a divorce at the moment. I am not sure this is the right time for her to take on more responsibilities," or "Given that she has recently become a single parent, we may want to give her more time to adjust and consider her for promotion during our next round."

Unfortunately, assumptions about one's ability to succeed despite setbacks still take place within the corporate environment, particularly for women. Leaders need to give individuals who are experiencing life-changing events the opportunity to dictate what can and cannot work for them. Making assumptions about their capabilities or bandwidth is detrimental to a working environment and organizational culture, and just plain wrong. Whether it is a decision about a divorce, choosing to become a single mother, or any decision that is considered outside the norm, biases exist. And in some cases, those biases can have an impact on opportunities.

We have all heard the term "It takes a village." The concept of the village is a beautiful one, a community of people who engage and extend themselves to help you manage your obligations. However, you can only reap the benefits of the village if you choose to ask for and accept help. Some people, including me, find it extremely difficult, but it's critical to solving for life's interruptions. Many of us shudder at the mere thought of asking for help. We may believe that asking for help is a sign of weakness, or that it is bothersome to other people, or that it requires giving up control. We are cognizant of the negative labels placed on us, particularly of being less competent because of the diversity we represent. It's no wonder that so many women of color struggle with seeking help. But you must recognize that not asking for the help you need becomes detrimental to all you have achieved and aspire to accomplish.

Tapping into the Village

I had been scheduled to lead a team at a conference that was crucial to our entry-level diversity hiring goals, and it required me to travel. My daughter was 10 years old at the time, and my usual go-to support system was not available to watch her for the duration of the four-day trip. I needed to be at the conference because, in my mind, no one would be able to lead the way I knew I could. I had to figure out a way to make it work.

I composed a message to my leader asking if I could bring my daughter to the conference, took a deep breath, and pressed the send key. Just like that, I had taken a risk in asking for help and there was no turning back.

I could feel his initial discomfort with the request when I met with him the next morning. He said nothing for quite a while, but we already know that I don't break uncomfortable silence. He finally said, "Nellie, I understand your situation, but it is not a usual thing for us to solve for this. I'll allow this, but only this once." I had been driven to ask for this accommodation because

I knew my lead was a supporter of mine. I also knew that, in my new role as a single parent, I had to advocate for what I needed to make my professional life work. There is power in knowing that your leader values you and your skills. By delivering consistently, you position yourself to better challenge the status quo due to your undeniable credibility.

This was one of the many asks I had during my seven-year journey as a single working mother. Though I consistently gave my all to ensuring Ginaly's well-being, I often experienced guilt about disrupting her family life. I ultimately concluded that it was the best decision I could have made for her and for me.

> *I was grounded on the principle that I earned the trust and support of my leaders, but it was up to me to leverage that and confidently ask for what I needed, no matter how uncomfortable it may have felt.*

Change doesn't typically happen if people don't ask for it, and I have always been comfortable in the role of a change agent. A former colleague, when confiding in me about her own challenges as a single mother in the corporate environment, said that no matter how difficult things got, she knew she could get through it because she had watched me get through it. What a testament to the positive influence we can have in others' lives through the things we are willing to be transparent about within the workplace. Anyone can have inner sadness, personal struggles, loss, or pain. Yet we expect them to deliver at the top of their game every single day. During this critical time in my daughter's life, I chose to ask for what I needed. I asked for flexibility to work from home on days when she was sick. Today, we experience more flexibility within our evolved work cultures but this was far from common back then. I learned to ask for what I needed while raising my daughter and adding continuous value to the organization. I was grounded on the principle that I earned the trust and support of my leaders, but it was up to me to leverage that and confidently ask for what I needed, no matter how uncomfortable it may have felt.

The thought of someone doing me a favor without me paying them back was completely foreign to me. Just as beliefs about asking for help take over our thoughts, so do hesitations about accepting help: How do I show my appreciation? How can I reciprocate the favor? How quickly can I showcase how grateful I am? Saying thank you and accepting the favor is simply enough sometimes, so why is it so hard for us to just sit back and be okay with that? For me, it's that lingering belief that tapping into someone's time translates to "bothering" them, and who likes to be bothered—no one! But I finally realized that not accepting the help was not only hurting me and my goals, but it was also depriving others of the opportunity to give of themselves in that part of my journey. So a mind shift was required.

Beautiful and Challenging Surprises

Driving into the New York office on the heels of multiple weeks of travel, I found myself tired and missing something. I couldn't pinpoint what it was, but it was an extremely strong emotion. I had consumed myself in everything Accenture. My career had spilled into my social life, which was easy to do because I worked with great people. We loved working together in the office and socializing outside of work, too. You know that saying, "Work hard; play hard"? We excelled at both.

As I drove into the office, I rolled the windows down to feel the refreshing breeze. The weather was perfect, and I had the radio volume blasting. Two songs came on, reminding me of clubbing with my friends back in the day. As the nostalgia of those simpler days set in, I realized I needed to reengage with my friends outside of my professional circle, to have moments not directly tied to my professional identity and relive my carefree days with them. In an effort to do so, I contacted a friend and said, "Let's get the group together for a reunion." In typical Accenture strategy planning mode, I scheduled a dinner to begin the event planning conversations. I had all the key points we needed to discuss, an established timeline, and what to focus on to make this reunion a reality. What I didn't plan for, or expect, was to make a love connection.

At the dinner table a few weeks later, my eyes immediately fixated on Ken, whom I had not liked in our friend group in our twenties, but who now looked quite impressive in professional stylish attire. They say life is filled with surprises, and in that moment, I felt like I was experiencing a very pleasant surprise with Ken. One year later, he presented me with a beautiful engagement ring and my daughter with a toe ring—too cute. We eloped to the Florida Keys where we were married with two total strangers as our witnesses—it was perfect!

A year into our marriage, we were doing great as a couple. We had found our perfect home, and the three of us settled in very nicely. My career was thriving, and everything aligned. So when the doctor told me I was pregnant, and quite far along in the pregnancy, I had an initial moment of panic. Ken was thrilled to hear the news, and so was I. But that inner voice started reverberating negativity, fear, and doubt, even as I gently touched my belly and fell in love with my new child.

Too many times, I hear women say, "I am pregnant, but I believe it will negatively impact my career, so I want to keep it hidden for as long as I can." For years, I coached women through the process of having this conversation with their leaders. I helped them move from a place of believing that pregnancy would negatively impact their trajectory to a place of celebrating this new phase of their journey instead. And yet, no matter how many times I had coached other women, I struggled to apply those key messages to myself.

My pregnancy progressed normally until about six months. That moment when you see abnormal spotting, your heart sinks and all you want to desperately know is that the baby is fine. At that moment, it does not matter if stepping away to have a baby prolongs a promotion. It doesn't matter that you don't know how time away will impact your career. All that matters is not losing your baby. I was put on bed rest. I heard loudly and clearly that I needed to rest, reduce stress, and simply relax in order to avoid premature labor. What was not clear to me was how others defined "relax." I found it stressful not to be on top of my work projects, leading the team, reviewing presentations, actively listening and advocating for people. So I kept working from my comfy sofa in my family room. I thought I was following my doctor's orders by not commuting into the office. Then the spotting intensified. That earned me a bed in a hospital room, as I lost the privilege of working from the comfort of my home. So I did what I thought was the next best thing to stay on top of everything. I set up my office in the hospital room. I asked my husband to print materials and bring them to me when he came to visit each day. I was even taking calls from my hospital bed, while convincing myself that I was relaxing. I was not missing a beat at work and I had it under control, or so I thought. I was in complete denial that my actions might be impacting my pregnancy because, in my mind, what was the harm in focusing on work rather than watching television all day, as long as I did it while lying in a hospital bed?

Then one day I received a call from the US HR lead at the time. I was so happy to hear his voice and looked forward to whatever request he would have for me. I took the call ready to talk about timelines and all things necessary to deliver. But instead of making a request, he started the conversation this way: "Nellie, I am told you are in the hospital."

"Yep, but I have it all under control. Been taking calls. Presented on a call earlier today. All is good." I was feeling accomplished. Superwoman! Getting it all done!

"Nellie, the cemetery is full of dispensable people," he responded to my surprise. "I am calling to shut you down. I have instructed your team not to contact you for work-related stuff. I need you to take the time you need to focus on your health and your baby. No more work calls."

I was furious. In my mind, it was not his decision to make. It was mine. But reflecting back on it now, what incredible leadership on his part! As soon as he became aware of my actions, he reached out to share his concerns. The question was, why was I having such a difficult time disengaging? What was I trying to prove and to whom?

My beautiful son Kenny was born prematurely and though he was in the NICU, all signs pointed to a very healthy baby requiring minimal time there. I was so grateful to God, the doctors, the nurses, and all who had a hand in providing my son what he needed during his first few days of life. It was hard to leave him there when I was discharged, but Ken and I went back each day. I would bring breast milk that I pumped at home to make sure he stayed nourished, but I was finding it hard to pump enough. The guilt and pressure were quite intense. I wanted him to have the best, and the few ounces I was producing did not feel like the best.

One day, I was feeling incredibly stressed while sitting on my bed pumping milk, when I suddenly I felt a sharp pain in my chest. It was so intense that I nearly fell off of the bed. Upon taking the milk to the NICU, I immediately told one of the unit nurses about the sharp pain. She did a manual breast exam and told me that I needed to make an appointment with my doctor. Two days later, I got the diagnosis of breast cancer.

So many thoughts flooded my brain: Am I going to live to see my son grow up? How will this impact my daughter as she finishes her senior year in high school? How will this impact my parents and my ability to take care of everyone in my family? I threw myself on my husband and cried uncontrollably. He held me and said, "Nellie, this is not what we would have wanted, but it is not a death sentence, and we will get through this." They were the exact words that I needed to start my fight.

There were phases in the process of battling breast cancer, including acceptance, and identifying what needed to change and what should remain the same. But I was completely surprised by an emotion I was not expecting: embarrassment. I was the fixer, the one in control. And now I needed help. I was embarrassed to need help and not be able to live up to the expectations and roles I had set up for myself.

It turned out that giving birth to my son gifted me a rebirth in many ways. The tumor had been within my body for approximately two to three years and was not visible during mammograms. The impact of pumping breast milk allowed me to feel the tumor.

So many people reached out during that difficult time. They called, sent meals, and even came to hold my son so that I could rest. There were Accenture leaders who called to let me know I was missed, but each encouraged me to take the time I needed, while assuring me that I would be welcomed back with open arms when I was ready to return. Those calls gave me a sense of calmness and relief. My mom, dad, husband, daughter, and sister-in-law all stepped up in ways that I could not have ever imagined. I was beautifully lifted, and I learned eventually how to welcome and embrace all of it, slowly freeing myself of that feeling of embarrassment.

Then there were those who left me questioning their motive. Their unsolicited remarks carried a common theme, though camouflaged with a tone of care. I constantly heard statements and questions like, "Nellie, now that you have breast cancer, shouldn't this be a sign to slow down?" "Nellie, I would imagine that after going through this medical scare, you would think about leaving your job and staying at home to spend more time with your family."

For goodness sake, how is any of this helpful? More importantly, do people with negative intentions really believe that the receiver is not wise enough to see right through it? A medical scare should not stop you from dreaming or visualizing bigger opportunities. In fact, visualizing my family flourishing and me energetically expanding my career is what got me through my breast cancer journey. Don't let anyone put a damper on your vision based on their beliefs. We have the choice and the power to discard their opinions or negative intentions.

Almost a year after my diagnosis, I returned to work. It took me a while to get back into my rhythm. A lot had changed in such a short period of time. I had changed! But there is such power in those you surround yourself with. I was cheered on by my close network, each partnering with me until I was back in my groove and flow. Though I loved being back at work, I also longed to be at home taking care of my son. When I finally opened up in a conversation with a woman leader, she gave me some words of advice that I still carry with me. "Nellie, you need to choose to be okay with knowing you feel guilty, but devoting energy to the guilt is not helpful if it distracts you from your task at hand and being present." In other words, while at work, don't devote energy to feeling guilty about not being at home; and while at home, don't put any energy into feeling guilty about not being at work. It is not about choosing to dismiss or not acknowledge your feelings of guilt. It's about choosing what energy you will give it in order not to let it consume you. Be present in your current decision and situation, even if your go-to emotion is to feel guilty.

Her words were so timely. Just a few days before, I was in the kitchen cooking dinner while my daughter, who was home from college for the weekend, played with my son on the floor. After what seemed like a super-long workweek, I was so happy to be home and to see them together. Though it was Friday evening, I had my laptop open on the kitchen counter, and I was still getting emails. Every time I heard the ping of an email coming in, I would run to the laptop and look at it. It didn't matter what I was in the middle of doing, whether I was playing with them, mixing the sauce, or draining spaghetti. Every ping demanded my undivided immediate attention. After becoming somewhat frustrated with my constant distraction, my daughter said to me, "Mom, I have a question for you. Are you in competition with somebody at work?"

I thought that was the most ridiculous question, and I quickly fired back, "Why would you say that?"

"Well, I'm asking you that because every single time you get a ping from your laptop, you run to answer it. Do you have to answer before somebody else or something . . . because you claim to be present when you are home, but you don't seem that present to me right now."

Wow. It was a hard pill to swallow. I took a few minutes to let it sink in. She was right about so many things, but especially about not being present and wanting to be the first to respond to everything. I remember feeling so upset with myself at that moment. I could handle disappointing myself, but disappointing my kids was unacceptable to me. I had to ask myself why I felt the need to be the first one to answer every email, and recognize that, once again, this was all stemming from the belief that I needed to show up 110% better than anybody else. To prove my value. And in order to meet that goal, one of the ways to prove myself was being quick to respond no matter the day or time. Basically, I was always on. I needed to create boundaries and limits.

The guilt of being away starts to take form through different actions. As I began to pick up my travels again, managing it was a continuous challenge. I felt the need to control everything regarding my son when I was not home, even though I knew that he was in very capable and loving hands with my husband. It started with me creating color-coded agendas for every activity, school projects, or anything that required focus. Then I began to leave goody bags for every day I was gone. These bags were very well thought out and sophisticated. I decorated each of them with a theme and stuffed them with toys and my son's favorite snack. The effort was exhausting, but it made me feel better for a while. Then the night came when I found myself sitting on my family room floor at 2 a.m. decorating goody bags, despite the fact that I had an early morning flight. I knew there had to be a better way of dealing with my need to be perfect and present.

Upon my return from that trip, Kenny said to me in a very mature manner, "Mom, can you just start leaving Game Stop gift cards instead?" And that is exactly what I did. We each have to find our ways of addressing how we feel about our choices. I had to get comfortable with letting go of the pressures I was placing on myself. It took some discipline for me to develop mindfulness around being present and being okay with my decisions about managing my priorities. But it was a welcome game changer that I am still mindfully integrating today.

Choices

As your parents get older, you start to see the changes. The slower pace of walking or response to questions. Doctor's appointments become more frequent, and you find yourself trying to integrate them into your schedule. Then the day comes when your father falls ill, and your life is disrupted as you try to manage it all.

My father passed away within two weeks of being hospitalized. Within those two weeks, I was managing new territory: being strong for my mom as she was facing the loss of her husband of more than 50 years, being present for my dad as he faced his transition, ensuring my daughter and son would be able to emotionally handle the loss of such a giant in their lives, and leveraging my professional network to step in for me as I needed to step out. I was in autopilot mode getting it all done.

I witnessed my father's valor and calmness in awe as he took his last breath. My heart was broken, and grief consumed me. But I went into the mode of solving for everyone's emotions and bringing the family together to celebrate his life. My biggest cheerleader was physically gone. I felt a tremendous loss, but one I could not dwell on because I now had a new concern to address. How would I make sure that my mother was okay?

A year later, we were in my car heading towards the shopping mall when she shared with me that she had been feeling off health-wise. I immediately called to schedule an appointment with her doctor, which led to another appointment and another appointment. I was as busy as ever with my professional responsibilities, but I worked out my schedule in order to be at each of them. One particular appointment conflicted with a program I was leading in London. I contemplated whether or not I should go, but my husband volunteered to take my mom to the appointment.

The first day of the program was a success and I felt good upon my return to the hotel room after dinner. Then I received a text from Ken asking if I could talk. It wasn't his usual cheery text, and I immediately sat down sensing something was wrong. I called him, and my body trembled as I heard him say the words "Your mom has been diagnosed with bladder cancer." It was a moment of choice. Do I stay in London three more days, or do I head home to hug my mom right away and let her know we will fight this together? It didn't take me long to choose the latter, and I was on a flight back home the next day. My colleagues quickly stepped in to fill the gap. That is the power of working with incredible people, those colleagues who quickly support you even when it means they need to take on more. This is not to be taken for granted in every organization. I feel fortunate to be part of a culture where I have mutually supportive colleagues. This is the result of choosing to engage authentically and build nurturing relationships.

I know that some will question why I needed to debate a decision at all. Of course, my immediate instinct was to prioritize my mother, but there was also a part of me that knew I was about to step away from the professional moments that were important to me as well. There can be a sense of missing out when we have to mindfully integrate our personal and professional lives, but the key is considering what you would rather miss out on. For me, not being present for my mom during a moment that undoubtedly was scary and difficult for her was not a choice I was willing to make.

My mother battled cancer for five years, enduring painful exams, surgeries, and chemo. She did it with incredible strength and grace, and I was fully present for her journey. Today, as I write this book, my mom is 88 years old and in remission. I have zero regret when I prioritize my mom. She is my pillar of strength and my greatest mentor, so I need her to feel supported and cared for at all times. I never want to make her feel as if she is keeping me from my professional responsibilities. But some days I still struggle with the process of being pulled in different directions. I have to be very intentional about what gets my attention, so I leverage every moment I can, including those times when I am stuck in New York City traffic traveling between my mother's doctor appointments and taking a work conference call while in my car. We have to figure out how to make it work, and we also have to release ourselves from guilt. And choosing my mom and her health absolutely relieves me from my guilt.

Adapt to the Unplanned

My daughter had accepted a great role at a technology company on the West Coast, and I was having a total meltdown as I drove back from dropping her off at the airport. Fortunately, that difficult day was followed by many amazing trips to visit Ginaly in California. We always had so much fun and I cherished those opportunities to spend time together, even if the visits always ended with both of us crying as we said goodbye. So when the lockdown of the global pandemic hit close to home, I knew that it would impact my ability to visit Ginaly. That was one of the many harsh realities of Covid-19, and it made me very sad. But I had no idea early on how sad I would eventually become.

Ginaly became pregnant during the pandemic. She and Ronald were beyond thrilled, and we were all ecstatic for them as well. I hated that I could not be there to cook for her cravings and help her during her pregnancy, but we did craft a plan so that I could be present for the birth of my first grandchild. With all of the Covid restrictions in place, we decided the best course of action was for me to fly to California, rent a short-term apartment, quarantine for 14 days, get tested, and then enter her "bubble." We timed it to coincide perfectly with her due date, and I could not wait to get through my quarantine period so I could hug her and touch her belly!

On December 20, 2020, I headed to the airport to catch an early flight. I was not feeling well but I had just received a negative Covid test result two days earlier. As I was standing in line to check my luggage, I received a call from Ronald telling me that Ginaly was in labor. "What!? What do you mean!? She's not due for another three weeks!" I went into full panic mode. Our timing was off now. I would not be able to be with her when she returned home as I would need to quarantine for those 14 days. I sat on that flight from Newark to San Francisco, double masked, with goggles, a face shield, and gloves. Not a sip of water, not a bite to eat. I was determined to minimize my risk of catching Covid. It felt like the longest flight ever as my mind raced with anxiety about not being there for Ginaly while she was in labor. I so wanted to be there.

Liam Phoenix Rodriguez was born later that evening, beautiful and healthy. The next morning, I felt extremely tired and weak, with a cough. My husband called to tell me that he also was not feeling well and was on his way to get tested. Within a few hours, he shared that he tested positive. Sheer panic set in. My mind raced with worries about my teenage son back home getting sick as well. Would they be okay? I worried about myself. Heck, did I have Covid? I knew I would need help, so I reached out to Accenture's Chief Leadership and Human Resources Officer, Ellyn Shook. I sent her a text detailing my current reality.

She immediately responded, "Don't panic. I will call you in ten minutes." It was exactly what I needed to hear in that moment filled with anxiety. I instantly stopped panicking, as Ellyn went into support mode. She rallied a team to provide me with everything I needed, from testing and food to emotional support.

The Accenture team also provided daily meals back at home for my husband and son, who ultimately did test positive. I am eternally grateful for the incredible level of outreach we received. Ellyn, along with other colleagues and leaders, showcased their truly human spirit.

After testing positive, I spent three weeks in that apartment, pushing myself each day to stay physically strong. There were definitely some bad times, like the day my vision became so blurry that I thought I had lost my eyesight. And I was a hot mess emotionally. I felt terrible for not being there to help my daughter during the first few weeks after giving birth. I felt guilty for not being with my son and husband while they battled Covid. The reality of my son being ill without me there to care for him was an unbearable pain.

Once cleared, I met my daughter outside. I gave her a huge hug as tears flowed uncontrollably down my face. When I pulled away, I said, "These are not tears of sadness, they are tears of joy that I finally get to see you and meet my grandson." The birth of my first grandchild was nowhere near what I had dreamed, but it was a life-changing experience on so many levels. After a total of five weeks in California, I boarded a plane, double masked, with goggles, a face shield, and gloves again to fly home. It is so hard to want to be in two places. My heart broke as I left my daughter and grandson. But it was also filled with joy and excitement to see my husband, my son, and my mom. I was so grateful for my recovery, as well as the recovery of my husband and my son. As I hugged them that day, I held on a little longer and tighter than usual.

The difficulty of asking for help through personal challenges and disruptions often requires an internal dialogue. We must create the space to contemplate the benefits of seeking the support we need. We must also believe that we earned the opportunity to be supported during these challenges in our journeys. And we need to identify what our ideal support looks like and whether that support is available to us. Once we do this internal contemplation, we can reach out for help.

Integrate Mindfully

I have never embraced the term "work–life balance." I know this is meant to inspire a healthier lifestyle, but to me it has always felt more like a reminder of how unbalanced we often feel. Instead, I think of it as mindfully integrating the various aspects of my personal life and my work life. There may never be a perfect balance. But I can thoughtfully choose what my priorities will be on any given day, week, month, or year. I will choose what to outsource versus what I personally commit to. I will weigh the pros and cons of decisions that conflict with my personal and professional life.

As I think about the reasons why I prioritized work while on bed rest or while at home with my kids, I realize that I was driven by my fear of losing ground and the success I had created for myself. I wanted to ensure that no one could lose sight of the value I added. That was a lot of worry to carry, but it also made me more mindful of the challenges others face as well. There is so much for us to think about when managing teams, working with colleagues, and engaging with our own leadership. When life events have impacted their routines, are we choosing to pause and recognize their pain points and the internal conflicts they are experiencing? Are we operating as a truly human leader when they lose a loved one? Are we aware that a person going through medical challenges may be fearful of the impact it will have on their livelihood and career?

The interruptions to my professional plan have each influenced my personal and professional growth, positioning me to move on during those moments when sacrifices felt too daunting. I learned how to recognize those moments when I needed to persuade myself to stop doubting my choices and instead embrace them and trust that they were the right decisions for me at the time. I have gained a clearer understanding of the importance in creating a safe space and encouraging people to share their feelings and true circumstances when experiencing complex life events, because it is through those conversations that their real needs come to light. I have also learned not to wait for people to ask me for help because I know how difficult that is for many to do. Instead, I simply offer. I have also realized the gift I give to others when I welcome their help instead of denying them the opportunity to engage with me in those challenging parts of my journey. Interruptions happen, but a plan interrupted can still be a successful and beautiful plan!

Questions for Consideration

1. In what ways do you hesitate to ask for and accept help at work?

2. What steps are you taking to prioritize unexpected life events over work-related responsibilities?

3. How can you help build a more mindful and supporting environment for yourself and your colleagues at work?

6

Asserting Yourself Through Your Brand

As a frequent participant on panels, I often hear this question: "What word best describes you?" I have heard a wide range of responses from fellow panelists. Hopeful, passionate, motivated, determined, and resilient are among the most common. And while I can align with all of these, my response is always "Courageous." There are a few ways to define this word, but the one that best drives my connection with it is this: "having or showing the ability to meet danger and difficulties with firmness." That one line encompasses exactly what it takes to navigate through change. There have been times when my decisions have been "dangerous" to my career. I would question how they might impact my performance evaluation or promotion prospects. And there have been times when the journey has been difficult. After all, not everyone was aligned to the change I was advocating. But every step of my journey has required firmness in my decisions with no turning back. It has required finding those incredible leaders, colleagues, and peers who were on board to support the platform I was representing and aiming to deliver on.

My Brand of Courage

I received a text message late in the evening from a mentee who had recently risen to a leadership role saying, "Time for a quick chat?" The conversation was familiar to what I have heard from other women of color: "I'm being told by one of the leaders that she is supportive of me in my new role. Yet each idea or proposal that I tee up, she immediately shoots down. Her messages are inconsistent, and I want to address this but I'm not sure what to do. I'm frustrated by her condescending attitude and disingenuous intent to support."

I think of my personal brand, Courage, as an evolution of my reputation. Like my reputation, I value my brand because it allows me to take some intentional ownership over how I want to be seen and experienced by others. I am a big fan of those who successfully create and effectively position their own, and I attribute a lot of my success to defining, executing, and fiercely protecting the brand I created for myself.

Tapping into my own brand for guidance, I asked my mentee, "What is your brand?"

She proudly responded, "Being balanced. I am balanced in every decision."

I followed up by asking her, "Is being balanced positioning you to show up in an assertive, confident, and savvy way? Is it reminding you to claim your space and nudging you to pull from your emotional intelligence? How is your brand helping you decipher how you should be responding to this leader who is delivering mixed messages?"

I knew early in my career that it was going to take courage to navigate through a culture that was not designed for my success. It was going to take courage to speak up for myself and advocate for others. It was going to take courage to challenge the status quo. And it was going to take a whole lot of courage to travel around the world and execute on an agenda of inclusion. My brand has been my consistent compass through all of it. When I am contemplating whether a decision is too risky, I rely on my brand. When I am doubting an

When you fail to craft your individual brand, you deprive yourself of the opportunity to show up in the way you want to be seen.

action I want to pursue, I rely on my brand. Even when my negative inner voice wants to loudly remind me that I don't belong, I rely on my brand. I have constantly reminded myself to trust and live through my brand of courage, and I can't imagine my journey without that foundation.

During my conversation with my mentee, it was clear to me that she had not created a brand that she could pull from when experiencing challenging times. Yes, being balanced is a great attribute, but for many members of diverse communities, we need a brand that reminds us of our inner strength and that positions us to be viewed by others as someone to be respected, valued, and maybe even admired. Getting there takes planning, nurturing, and the ability to consistently display what your brand represents. Think about what you want to be known for. The brand you establish will, in many circumstances, dictate how others engage with you, while the absence of a brand can open the door to others' attempts to influence how you are viewed. When you fail to craft your individual brand, you deprive yourself of the opportunity to show up in the way you want to be seen.

Integrating Your Brand with Your Power

I was leading a diversity course outside of the US that focused on the challenges of a particular ethnic group. We had created a safe and engaging space by which we could openly talk about the obstacles, as well as the opportunities, for this community of color. Senior leaders joined for portions of the program, and as we were preparing for a very senior leader to present his commitment to diversity, I asked each participant to think about questions they wanted to ask him.

After introducing the leader, I grabbed a seat where he and I had a clear view of each other. I was feeling so incredibly proud of the progress we were all making and how this particular focus had rapidly evolved. Then the leader was asked a question that visibly stumped him. The participants wanted specifics about which two or three things the organization would prioritize to close existing gaps. I could see and hear his discomfort as he tried to respond. He glanced in my direction with a plea for help. My heart started to race. I needed to quickly decide what my role would be in that moment. Would I jump in and help him answer the question, or would I sit back and give him an opportunity to work through it on his own? I decided to align with my brand of courage and not step in to answer the question for this leader, who was more senior than me.

To my relief, he eventually worked through his response in a very impressive way. After he wrapped up his presentation, I got up to thank him and escort him out. As we exited the room he asked, "Just curious, why didn't you step in to help me answer the question?"

I stopped, looked at him, and said, "I know it felt uncomfortable, but had I stepped in, it would have taken away from your credibility and it would not have given you an opportunity to position yourself as accountable for prioritizing your commitment to diversity." He nodded in agreement.

Two things happened during that experience. First, I adhered to my brand. Second, as a senior executive, I recognized my power to choose not to step in. I solved for the participants of the program in that moment by getting a clear response from their leader instead. When you integrate your brand with your power, the result will always be impactful outcomes.

As a person of color, I am aware that any decision I make towards embracing programs or people representative of my ethnicity will inevitably attract scrutiny from others outside of my demographic. We must constantly defend our decisions and prove their unbiased validity, and once again, the level of energy this requires could be better aligned elsewhere. But unfortunately, many people of color often feel pressured to justify actions that may be viewed as excluding nondiverse groups, when what they are really doing is creating a path towards closing gaps. To that, I say: don't be swayed! Such was the case when I decided to include HBCUs and Hispanic Serving Institutions (HSIs) into our recruiting target schools.

I knew that one particular school would raise some eyebrows, not for justifiable business reasons, but rather for invalid assumptions. That school was the University of Puerto Rico—Mayaguez, a school that had and continues to have a high-caliber accredited engineering program, and therefore the potential to bring in amazing talent to the company. Yet that part was ignored, and I was continuously questioned for the choice. Given the pushback, it would've been so much easier for me not to select this school, but I was convinced and felt assured that we would tap into great talent there. I knew that not only would we hire excellent technical majors, but we would also increase our Hispanic representation. I had a bigger vision not only to target this one school in Puerto Rico but also to expand to other universities on the island as well. With that as my credible basis, I set out to face the less than pleasant commentary. I constantly heard questions like, "Nellie, are you just looking to go visit your family in Puerto Rico and have a vacation?" or "Will they meet our standards?" I was also asked, "Are they US citizens?" The list was long.

Because of this, I was cautious with every move I made. I didn't dare tag an extra day onto my travel to Puerto Rico, even at my own personal expense, to see my parents, who at the time lived on the island and would always ask me to stay a day or two. Instead, they would drive to the airport and see me for a few hours before I departed. I knew the scrutiny that I was under, which still makes me sad to this day. I am sure that I had colleagues at the time who recruited at their alma maters or schools located near their families and would, without hesitation or fear, tag on days to visit with friends or family. I didn't feel that I had the same privilege.

I also felt the added pressure of ensuring that each hire was successful. I had a constant concern that even a single negative experience would look bad, not only on me, but on every other recruit from the school. The pressure was exhausting, but the ultimate rewards were so worth it. Not only did we hire excellent talent from the University of Puerto Rico—Mayaguez, but we also expanded to multiple schools on the island. Today, we have incredible talent within our organization from those universities, inclusive of all the HBCUs we targeted as well. All of this wouldn't have been possible if I hadn't stuck to my beliefs and leveraged my brand of courage to bring in these amazing new recruits.

Different Setting, Same Brand

I was sitting in a large conference room with the senior leadership of a client. I had been asked by their HR leader to come in and help solve a very public diversity-related incident. The tension in the room was palpable. The only other person of color in the room from their organization was a junior executive with limited influence. I intently listened to how the organizational brand was going to be impacted, and there were many things to solve for. For starters, there was the recognition that they needed a business-driven focus on diversity. I sensed that these were all good people who were finally realizing that they were in need of a cultural shift. I listened as I waited for the perfect moment to insert my thoughts into the conversation. When I spoke, my approach was direct and assertive. I didn't want to sugarcoat the impact this diversity incident was having on their customer base. But where I really placed my focus was on their employees. I put a few challenging questions on the table: How is this impacting your employee base? Will some opt to leave because of this incident? How is this going to impact their employee engagement and the pride they felt from being aligned with their organization? How quickly could a communication be sent to explain how the organization would address the issue?

As I continued, I could feel the discomfort in the room. They wanted to give their most senior leader more time to process the questions I had posed and think through his response, but I knew that time was of the essence, and I wanted everyone to feel the intensity of the moment. So I courageously continued pushing without hesitation. It was not easy, but we eventually came up with a good plan for connecting with the employees, and I was relentless in leading us there. I had taken two colleagues with me to the meeting, and as we walked out, one said, "Nellie, wow, that was intense but brilliantly impactful. I could not have handled the meeting in the way that you did."

I responded, "I am who I am no matter where I am." In that moment, I had confirmed two things for myself. The first was that I am deeply passionate about solving for people and I knew the employees of this organization needed attention. Second,

I am driven by courage, even when out of my comfort zone. That was the moment when I saw a glimpse of how I had sold myself short throughout the years with my belief that positioning my expertise as a client market offering was not for me.

There have been many client experiences over the years that have shown me how necessary it is to have bold leaders step in and advocate for their employees. I even had one meeting where I was the only person of color in a room of very disengaged attendees. In that meeting, I could've opted to simply move on with my presentation as planned. I could've told myself to ignore their disinterest and simply get through it. But that would not be me. Instead, I courageously acknowledged the disengagement in the room, challenging them to think about why HR had brought me in to talk to them. I recognized that I had been hired to help these leaders understand the impact of diversity and that was exactly what I was going to do, even if it meant that we were all going to be a little uncomfortable before we got comfortable.

Setting Boundaries by Recognizing Your Brand

I was looking forward to catching up with a long-time friend, another Latina executive, who is a devout Catholic. We were both just coming back from the Easter holiday when we jumped on a video call. I quickly sensed her heaviness, as it was clear that something was bothering her. I mentioned how much I loved her social media post of her Easter Sunday family pictures and said, "It looks like you had a beautiful and relaxing Easter weekend."

She responded, "No, I did not. As a matter of fact, I am feeling anxious and angry about it."

I could see the anger and sadness on her face. I paused for a few seconds, wanting to give her the space to work through her emotions. She began sharing that her leader tried reaching out to her several times via her personal mobile phone on Good Friday, which is considered one of the most sacred Christian holidays. She ignored the first two incoming calls, which had already caused her some level of anxiety. By the third call, she opted to pick up and respond. In her mind, the ask from the leader was not urgent and could have waited. She was annoyed by the interruption to her holy Friday, where disengaging from work is a part of the observance. She continued to share that numerous emails were also coming in throughout the weekend and that she felt compelled to respond to an email on Easter Sunday. She said that she was very confused about where to properly align her anger. Was it with her leader, herself, or both?

Now, many readers may decide that it was her fault for making herself available, while others will say that her leader displayed poor leadership judgment. Both of these perspectives have some validity, but those were not my first observations. Instead, I asked, "What made you feel that you needed to pick up that call and respond to that email? I know you, and I know how devoted you are to your faith, which leads me to believe that you are not feeling secure enough in your role if you dropped the sacredness of your holy day to respond." She knew that she allowed her leader to cross some boundaries, and I advised her to address them with her leader so that they are not crossed again. And in addition to sticking to her boundaries, she would also give her leader the opportunity to grow from this and be more mindful of boundaries with her team members.

I could see that there was an internal debate going on within her. She was emotional because she felt that she had betrayed her faith by making herself available to her leader. But she wanted her leader to feel supported. And she didn't know how to talk to her about it without making her think she wasn't flexible. She wasn't feeling safe in her role, as I had inferred.

Understanding her concerns, I said, "I know how assertive and confident you can be. In fact, your brand is one of being direct and transparent. Are you willing to ignore your brand? Are you willing to let your brand be diluted by not acting in accordance with it?"

As we continued our discussion, she agreed to pull strength from her own brand and solve for several things, starting with having the conversation with her leader. We rehearsed her lines and determined that one specifically was a must: "I am bringing this to your attention because I want us both to evolve as better executives and leaders." In other words, raising the concern was not about who owns the blame. Rather, it was about how you can take an unpleasant experience and agree to mutually learn and evolve.

Leaders need to be aware that when they don't take into account the boundaries required for a healthy and supportive diverse work environment, they cause unnecessary disruption and anxiety for others. This often leads to a culture of depleted team members. Additionally, becoming familiar with religious observances across multiple faiths is an example of how leaders can support a culture of inclusion, as well as be an impactful ally.

Bring Everyone In, Lift Everyone Up

I was asked to join a meeting with an organization that was under significant pressure to increase their diversity representation. I was not invited by the DE&I lead, but rather the invitation was extended by a business leader. The room was quite full of various leaders, but as the conversation evolved, the silence from the DE&I practitioner concerned me. She had likely spent a lot of time building and upholding a diversity program for the organization, yet it appeared that her opinions as a subject matter expert were devalued by members of the leadership team. I understood how deflating that could feel.

Halfway into the meeting, I asked that we quickly and collectively list the areas of the business where we felt needed to be held accountable for doing more. After receiving a quick consensus, I turned to the DE&I practitioner and said, "I have a view of the top three things required to address the gaps, but before I share that, I would welcome your thoughts as to what the leadership team needs to stop doing, start doing, and continue doing in order to position everyone to successfully achieve the common goal." At that moment, I chose to bring her in. I chose to let her know that, as a fellow DE&I practitioner, I was going to give her the space to shine as well. It was now up to her to embrace that moment and leverage it. I followed my statement to her by adding, "It is important for this leadership team to understand what will be required to help you successfully lead alongside them."

I knew I had a choice to make. I could have simply positioned my expertise, or I could have made it a teachable moment. The opportunity to lead by example and create greater awareness about how to be an inclusive leader was not an opening I was willing to forgo. I wanted to infuse part of my courageous brand into the DE&I practitioner at that moment. I also wanted to showcase to the leadership team how to acknowledge that there were exclusionary behaviors being displayed.

I don't take for granted the platform I have to impact change or motivate others. I also understand and have gotten comfortable with choosing to be bold when feeling the most vulnerable. Crafting and reshaping one's brand should be an ongoing evolution. Think about what you want your image to be and whether your current brand continues to serve you as you have grown and evolved in your journey. Does it need to be tweaked in any way? Our career journeys take us through many twists and turns. Each experience gives us an opportunity to assess how we are showing up and what needs to be tweaked. For me, the fundamental essence of my brand has never faltered. I always have been and always will be courageous. But at different times, I have had to infuse different components into my brand in order to meet new goals or navigate through unfamiliar spaces.

Choose your brand wisely. One that will guide you and stretch you to enable you to reach your goal. A brand that will make you proud of you. The brand that will serve as your reliable compass. You have to be thoughtful about how your brand is serving you as you shift, grow, and evolve authentically. I am strongly suggesting that we benefit from having an awareness about the culture we are operating in. Once we have intentionally paused to fully understand our current setting and landscape, that awareness helps us decipher what actions we need to take in order to reach our goals. Creating and crafting our brand with that corporate cultural awareness in mind positions us to thoughtfully own how we will engage and sets the tone for how we choose to be viewed.

Every new level should include an assessment of how your brand has served you thus far, how it needs to serve you in the present, and what modification may be required to achieve future goals. The fundamental and foundational aspect of your brand should remain steady but have the flexibility to incorporate components that lend themselves to the evolution of your career and aspirations.

Questions for Consideration

1. What is your brand?
2. In what ways are you consistently executing against your brand?
3. How does your personal brand impact your career?

Solving for Self and Clients: Assessing Diversity, Equity, and Inclusion

Don't get mad, get creative. As I witnessed leadership changing and shifting towards a new direction, one troubling thought kept playing over and over in my head: "I need to relocate myself." It wasn't about going to a new city or a new home; it was about my role and my status. The intensity of the disruption that was about to take place, along with the sense of incredible unease that I felt, led me to recognize the need to relocate myself to a new role. I purposely chose not to use the word "change." It felt much heavier and certainly more threatening than that. I wasn't calmly telling myself that I needed to consider changing roles. In my mind, I was facing a huge disruption that left me feeling displaced with no other option but to uproot myself and create a new path—a theme that was quite familiar to me. Throughout my journey with Accenture, I had created every one of my roles, and here I was needing to do it again.

At first, I was not ready for the leadership changes that were taking place and I initially resisted them. Then one day I found myself feeling mentally, emotionally, and physically tired. I asked myself, "If one of your mentees was going through this experience, how would you help them?" That simple question allowed me to switch my perspective from one based in emotion to one based in reason, and I knew exactly what questions I would ask:

- What are you processing at this moment?
- Are you processing the change through a broader and holistic lens or are you more comfortable with the easier option of just sitting in the vacuum of anger and resistance?
- Do you realize that these changes are going to happen whether you resist them or not?

Considering these questions was a real *aha* moment for me. It shed clarity over the situation as I realized that my anger wasn't hurting anyone but me. And what benefit was I gaining by allowing my emotions to dictate my actions? I chose to pause and deal with my own feelings. This shift in mindset led me to ask myself a different set of questions:

- What if these changes are exactly what I needed, as well as what the organization needed to continue to evolve?
- What was behind my resistance?
- Is there ego or pride involved here? (This was a tough one.)

Being thoughtful about these questions and facing my feelings provided me with a real liberating moment. It gave me the space to seek and welcome my own clarity, and with that clarity I was able to tap into my courage, get creative, and align my skills to go beyond the limitations that surrounded the role I was not ready to let go of. Yes, I needed to shift my role, but that did not have to be a bad thing even though it felt bad at the time. I needed to give myself permission to validate that feeling and move beyond it.

Changes are inevitable as organizations evolve. Most of us simply cannot escape that reality. Leaders change, teams change, and career trajectories change. It's constant. These changes may initially disrupt and muddle our state of being, as well as our planned or perceived futures. But we cannot let that dictate our responses. Instead, we must choose to mindfully experience changes within our organizations, and when we do, the shift towards a new direction often becomes clear.

While I have always been courageous about maximizing diversity internally at Accenture, I was hesitant to transition into the role of delivering DE&I work externally to clients. I wouldn't allocate space to think through this as a potential option because I had convinced myself that I would not be good at selling the work. I also told myself that it would be hard to gain access to industry leaders as a Latina woman, especially considering the prevalent bias associated with my diversity. However, life springs so many surprises and sometimes it is through those surprises that we are forced to step into places we would otherwise convince ourselves not to go.

I decided to be still and welcome the flow of possibilities that were now bouncing through my mind. It was not where I wanted or would've chosen to be in the moment, but it was my new reality and I needed to direct myself towards the new role of delivering DE&I work externally. As I said before, carving out a new role was familiar territory to me, but it did feel a lot different this time. This change was not because of me positioning myself to expand my scope or bringing leaders along to sponsor diversity programs throughout the world. I didn't have an exact playbook from previous experiences to rely on for my next step. There was no roadmap for what my next move should be in this new circumstance.

Many professionals find themselves in these types of situations. It's a part of facing organizational changes. In some cases, you will lead some of these changes and every decision you make will impact others. Then there will be organizational changes led by others where you will experience the impact. When this happens, you may feel like you are being displaced or personally wronged in some way, which is exactly how I felt. But there is something extremely important to remember in those moments . . . feelings can be destructive, leaving no room for the excitement that you could experience for the challenges and opportunities ahead.

This is not to say that we do not sometimes experience situations that justifiably lead us to doubt whether those with influence over our careers will choose to position us for continued success. However, we have a responsibility to ourselves to ensure that we are balancing our emotions and deciphering through the destructive noise. If we are not careful, that noise can lead us towards emotionally driven decisions, which ultimately do not us or the organization.

Shaping an inclusive culture can feel like heavy lifting, requiring courage for self-reflection and boldness to lead. I, and others, have undoubtedly taken risks as we have advocated for change. Creating and sustaining an inclusive culture that is felt by all employees and customers requires commitment, advocacy, and awareness related to the experiences of the various diversity segments. Simply having inclusion and diversity programs in place is not enough. The true success of inclusion and diversity goals towards equity and equality depends on the impact these programs are having for the employees. Are these programs moving the needle? Are they closing gaps across the talent life cycle: attracting, retaining, developing, and advancing talent? Are they evolving cultures and embracing the authenticity of the employees? Are they solving for talent equity?

Today, employees expect organizations to place significant priority on inclusion, diversity, equity, and equality, provoking business leaders to seek clarity on DE&I and how to effectively promote it within their organizations. Within Accenture, Carolina Cardoso, Johnathan Medina, and I led the creation of our DE&I market offering. Throughout our engagement across these organizations, we were posed these common questions. Employees asked, "Where do you believe my organization is in relation to their commitment to diversity and inclusion?" Leadership asked,

"Where do you believe we need to be to continue to demonstrate our commitment to diversity and inclusion?" These two questions, along with my experience at Accenture, led to the development of the Maturity DE&I Framework, which we share with clients to help them truly assess where they are and where they need to be in their DE&I goals.

The Four Pillars of the DE&I Maturity Framework

At Accenture, diversity encompasses all the visible and nonvisible ways people differ, including unique styles, experiences, identities, and ideas. Inclusion is an environment where differences are welcomed, valued, embraced, and celebrated. All people feel a sense of community and belonging. We define equity as the process of providing opportunity, access, and support to address imbalances and create fair, impartial treatment so that everyone can thrive. At Accenture, we position Inclusion first because we firmly believe that a culture of inclusion must be created in order to receive and retain diverse talent with an emphasis towards creating equity.

The Accenture Maturity Diversity, Equity & Inclusion (DE&I) Framework ranges from the very "basics" of meeting regulatory requirements to the "leading" practices that create a business differentiator. This model provides a clear way to assess organizational performance. Let's dig deeper into the assessment of each phase:

Phase I: Foundational (Right Thing to Do), Basic Actions:

- The organization views D&I as a method to monitor compliance.

- D&I Strategy exists in certain parts of the organization, but is not managed centrally.

- D&I Committee is established, but is led by mid-level resources with limited influence.

- Procurement processes loosely consider supplier diversity as part of a broader set of criteria.

- Employee Resource Groups (ERG) exist but do not have accountability for D&I goals.

- Communication on D&I is ERG-driven.

Phase II: Programmatic (Business Imperative), Intermediary Actions:

- D&I Strategy is managed centrally and is aligned to the business strategy.

- D&I business case is defined and tracked through specific metrics and leadership communicates D&I goals internally.

- D&I Committee evolves to a more formally governed structure as D&I Council that is responsible for D&I outcomes.

- Organizational policies are influenced by D&I Strategy.

- Supplier diversity is a component of the overall D&I Strategy.

- ERGs have clear D&I objectives and goals.

Phase III: Strategic (Business Accountability), Advanced Actions:

- D&I is integrated into the business strategy and supported by all functions, not just Human Resources.

- Leadership measures the impact of policies and actions in place to ensure they are supporting stated D&I goals.

- D&I Council is responsible for D&I outcomes, supported by D&I Lead, dedicated resources and championed by C-suite.
- Leaders can articulate the business case for D&I.
- D&I gaps in talent pipeline (beyond gender) are addressed and used to inform D&I Strategy and workplace practices.
- ERGs are funded and measured based on D&I outcomes.

Phase IV: Integrated and Sustainable (Business Responsibility), Leading Actions:

- All employees understand the business case for D&I and demonstrate inclusive behaviors.
- A diverse leadership team sets, measures, and shares D&I targets externally.
- Chief D&I Officer/Lead reports to C-Suite and is responsible for developing and implementing D&I strategies to the vision set by the D&I Council or overall, most senior organizational leadership.
- Leaders are accountable for reaching D&I goals.
- Functions/Business Units are measured on their contributions to D&I outcomes.
- Predictive analytics and debiasing tactics are used to foster diverse talent pipelines.
- ERGs operate as Business Resource Groups and are measured on business outcomes (e.g., product development, corporate branding).

As organizations continue to seek ways by which to successfully create a sustainable culture of inclusion, equality, and equity, they must be committed to imbedding D&I across these six key organizational focus areas:

- Strategic Intent, where inclusion and diversity are integrated in the organization's overall growth strategy and communicated throughout the organization

- Communications, where thoughtful and inclusive communications are essential to the success of the organization

- Metrics & Analytics, identify D&I goals through data-driven approach that identifies areas of improvement and tracks progress

- Leadership Behaviors, where leadership is held accountable to model behaviors that make those with different backgrounds feel welcomed, heard, and treated equally

- Talent Actions, align resources to attract, retain, develop, and advance talent programs to build diverse and inclusive teams throughout the organization

- Inclusive Culture, where people of all backgrounds and cultures feel included and valued

I proudly share that Accenture is in Phase IV, the Leading phase. Reaching this point has been the result of multiple leaders around the world believing in the business value and power of diversity. We prioritized moving beyond simply tolerating differences to embracing them and created an environment where authenticity is celebrated. When these beliefs and mindsets are at the center and core of how leaders lead, it sends a clear message of inclusion that permeates throughout the organization. CEOs set the tone, and I can confidently say that as I witnessed the support and evolution through George Shaheen, Joe Forehand, Bill Green, Pierre Nanterme, and currently Julie Sweet. Each progressively expanded the focus of diversity through their leadership and voices, which has intensified through each transition.

The Maturity Framework in Action

One exercise that I enjoy doing with clients involves gathering several of the organization's leaders in a room together. I ask them to look at the Maturity Framework and individually tell me where they believe the organization stands along the DE&I journey. Without fail, the answers are never consistently aligned. There are always some who believe their organization is further behind and others who believe it is further along. I am never surprised by this lack of commonality because I understand that each leader taps into their own personal and professional lived experiences when making these assessments.

One particular client leadership group meeting stands out in my memory. A vast majority of the leaders adamantly insisted that the organization was doing all it could, and more than expected, to support an inclusive culture. But the diverse leaders voiced a very different perspective. I gave them an opportunity to talk through it, to challenge each other, and listen to the differing opinions. Throughout the debate, I asked for examples of what the organization was doing well, as well as specific instances where more could be done. For those who felt the organization is doing all they can, I also asked them to contemplate whether employees who are members of underrepresented groups across ethnicity, sexual orientation, and other aspects of diversity would agree with their assessment.

Given that this organization was customer facing, I asked these leaders to also consider these questions:

1. Do you believe your customers expect more regarding your stance on diversity?

2. Is there a concern about taking a public stance on high-profile sensitive issues that may alienate some customers?

3. Is that potential concern impacting how you are assessing the organizations' stance and positioning on diversity?

4. Is the organization taking diversity into account when engaging with suppliers?

5. What expectations do you believe your shareholders have related to DE&I?

I intentionally raised these questions to drive home the point that a commitment to DE&I requires a broad view of all business angles, internal and external to the organization. As they talked, I observed how intently the CEO listened. His nonverbal cues gave no indication where he stood on the debate. I couldn't tell if I was looking at someone who was indifferent or genuinely focused. Though I wondered if his leadership team was being impacted by his silence, I was also impressed by the group's ability to disagree and have a passionate debate in the presence of the CEO.

After winding down the discussion, I looked over to the CEO for his response. He looked around the room and said, "Thank you all for this powerful dialogue. I would say that we are not doing enough, and we need to figure out how we balance supporting our employees, solving for our customers, and what we expect from our suppliers. We are barely at Phase II of this Maturity Model and we should all aim to reach Phase IV." He continued with his belief that there was ample opportunity to evolve before asking, "Is everyone ready to dig in and reach our new goals?" Every leader enthusiastically gave their support.

What a beautiful moment. The leadership team felt empowered to speak their minds and respectfully challenge each other. The CEO was graceful in giving them that space and displayed incredible leadership by acknowledging the inadequacies of the current state and setting a goal to aim for. Each leader understood they had just been tasked with making DE&I a priority for the organization and an important part of their leadership roles. The tone had been set at the very top. The CEO was viewing the advancement of DE&I as yielding business value, positively impacting the brand, customers, and workforce through innovation and growth.

We Can't Afford "Diversity Fatigue"

Several years ago, I was participating on an external diversity panel when one panelist ardently said, "You know, we're all experiencing diversity fatigue." The term was starting to pick up steam across many circles, but I wasn't willing to give this new trend any credibility. I saw it as an excuse for people who resented—or even opposed—conversations and actions that supported diverse communities. I wanted to jump in and quickly respond to the comment by my co-panelist. I took a deep long breath as if almost searching for patience before responding, "I am not experiencing diversity fatigue and I wish we would all remove that phrase from our conversations. As diversity practitioners, we do not have the luxury to experience 'diversity fatigue' or to give that statement any more credence. If the ones tasked to lead buy into that and accommodate others who subscribe to that, how in the world are we expecting to make progress and influence change?"

As I was responding, I was struck by the number of people in the audience nodding their heads in agreement. Though I was pleased to see their reaction, I was feeling the weight of my deliberate and assertive response. I had quickly spoken up because I felt an intense need to address my co-panelist's comment right there in the moment. However, when participating on panels, my goal is to always share the stage equally and be complimentary to my co-panelist. But choosing not to say something and letting this term continue to permeate throughout this conference would have been in direct conflict with my brand and what I stood for. I gently directed my attention toward her with an encouraging prompt for her to close out the topic. In return, she smiled at me and said, "You are right. Thank you!" It was a powerful moment.

DE&I practitioners who effectively lead take on a huge and critical role, which is undoubtedly key to the continued success of organizations. It is a wide scope combining strategic, operational, and human-centric engagement. As DE&I practitioners, we:

- Sponsor, encourage, influence, coach, motivate, advocate, mentor
- Speak up with courage and confidence
- Serve as confidants and trusted advisors
- Challenge norms and customs to reshape cultures and behaviors
- Create, design, and execute strategic programs
- Rally allies and supporters

- Educate, aiming to change hearts and minds
- Reach across communities and highlight intersectionality
- Enable our organizations to increase their business results
- Shake off setbacks, redirect and bounce back
- Represent and speak on behalf of our organizational brands
- Creatively identify ways to bring everyone along in the spirit of inclusion

To effectively deliver, we are required to be unwavering, relentless, and fully committed to our mandate towards reaching equity and equality. But another critical component to the success of the DE&I practitioners is the support and sponsorship of colleagues, peers, and most importantly leaders. DE&I practitioners should not be expected to carry the weight of it all on their own. Organizations need leaders who embrace DE&I as a priority within their agenda. Throughout my many conversations with DE&I practitioners across industries, I have found that many hesitate to take risks out of fear that the organization will not support their vision of what is truly required to effect the change. This is a disheartening reality. I hear comments such as, "My leadership does not really want to make changes," or "My leadership is more concerned about not upsetting those who feel excluded by targeted diversity programs." Then there are comments like, "My leadership does not want to take a stance prompting risks that may alienate our customer base" and "My leadership wants me to quantify expected results before approving resources to fund programs."

Engaged leadership helps speed up outcomes that would otherwise stall by leveraging their decision-making power to effect change.

The role of DE&I practitioner has shifted dramatically from being solely responsible for an organization's diversity results to sharing the responsibility with business leaders to enhance accountability. Together, leaders and DE&I practitioners leverage DE&I to create sustainable value, growth, and social impact. But in some cases, this has caused tension. DE&I practitioners have felt displaced by other business leaders who have taken on the role of speaking internally and externally about organizational DE&I commitments. I have had many external diversity peers reach out to me for advice when they have experienced the disruption of others stepping into what they perceive as their space. That has led to them feeling micromanaged or displaced. But I also understand the power of having leadership become more engaged in the diversity initiatives. When Ellyn Shook became our Chief Leadership and Human Resources Officer, she immediately set the tone that DE&I was the responsibility of every HR executive. She included DE&I as one of her top priorities and amplified her voice around it. This undoubtedly generated greater results. Engaged leadership helps speed up outcomes that would otherwise stall by leveraging their decision-making power to effect change. Through their leadership voice, they amplify the business imperative of prioritizing DE&I. For this reason, practitioners benefit from the engagement of leaders who have chosen to position DE&I as part of their platform and/or leadership responsibilities.

As a DE&I leader, you need to take time to define and create your brand. Will you be a leader who is known for courageously effecting change, increasing representation, and evolving a culture of inclusion? Or will you be a leader who positions your brand to be more externally focused, resulting in limited opportunities to maximize internal engagement and solve for diversity gaps? Will you be a leader who embraces collaboration?

It is not an easy role but understanding what you stand for and what you are willing to subscribe to provides you with a compass for how you are going to position yourself and your leadership.

Voices Amplified for Social Justice and Human Rights

I've been in the diversity space for over 30 years. I have experienced and have been a conduit to the evolution of the role globally and across industries. Today, DE&I practitioners are not only solving for internal diversity gaps. They also solve for much bigger, wider, institutionalized cultural and social inequity challenges. They are solving for broader human rights issues, social and racial injustices. In doing so, we have the opportunity to leverage the influence and power of the organizations we represent. That is an incredible role and responsibility.

When events reflective of social injustice touch and impact our lives, we experience fear for ourselves and our loved ones and in many cases go through our own grieving process. We don't need to necessarily know the impacted individuals, but we know the relatability associated with similarities, whether they are representative of our ethnicity, sexual orientation, religious affiliations, or any other trait that is experiencing hate-related actions or social injustices. To expect impacted people to show up to our workplaces as if nothing is happening is simply unrealistic. In addition, being in a space with people who don't view the injustices taking place as important weighs heavy on their hearts and minds.

For this reason, Accenture took a bold step in 2016 to create a platform we called Building Bridges. The program was designed to have an open dialogue on diversity because we believed it is important to provide a workplace where our people can have honest discussions about the social injustices that affect our colleagues, clients, family, friends, and communities. Our discussions have encompassed race and ethnicity, religion, LGBTQI+, and many other important topics. During these courageous conversations, people within diverse communities have shared their lived experiences with injustices all in the spirit of increasing the awareness and allyship of others.

While many organizations have started hosting their own "courageous" conversations, it is important to note the responsibility they have in ensuring that people who are voluntarily and openly sharing their lived experiences feel supported and not exposed to potential additional bias or hatred from any members within the organization. As we leverage their experiences to serve as an awareness and learning opportunity for others, we must make sure to provide any assistance they need, as they may be revisiting personal trauma.

We have created safe spaces for honest discussions on tough topics to build trust and increase transparency. We also scaled our country-specific Building Bridges program to local office "Listening Sessions" in an effort to create communities united by a purpose to solve for social injustices and issues. In 2020, the world witnessed the heartbreaking murder of George Floyd. This created a circumstance where it was imperative that I step away from client work to refocus on our internal organization. I was fully aware that the murder of George Floyd was about to spark a social reckoning and that people were hurting. I was hurting, but I knew that I would have to devote all my energy to leading the way. Three things needed to happen immediately:

1. I needed to gather the North America DE&I team to ask how everyone was feeling and provide them an opportunity to express their emotions, pain, fear, and hurt. I wanted to share with them that while we are each hurting, as representatives of the DE&I team, we would play a significant role in leading our organization through this ugly chapter of our American history.

2. I needed to bring together our highest-ranking African American leaders. I wanted to check in on each one and collectively come up with our approach as to how our organization should respond internally and externally.

3. I needed to connect with our C-level leadership—our CEO, CLHRO and other senior leaders. I was not surprised to discover that they were already in motion, impressively leading the way in determining how our influence and brand power would play a role in aiding in social and racial justice. So it was easy to align our roles and responsibilities in response to this social crisis. We were all united in pain and our fierce determination to be part of the change.

I devoted myself to being available to anyone or any group that needed to talk through what we were facing as a country, no matter what time of day or night. I wasn't sleeping well because I kept asking myself what more could I be doing. Quite honestly, I chose not to rest because I felt like it was my responsibility to be available. I was very aware that this level of intensity was not healthy or sustainable. I was in an internal battle. Then, one Sunday afternoon, while I was casually sweeping my family room, I felt myself growing anxious and angry. I was angry that we were still dealing with these issues in 2020. I was angry that someone's life had been taken. I was angry that I had to worry about my son, a young man of color. I was angry that women of color, and especially Black women, do not have the peace of mind about our sons' safety that other women have, and I was angry that some people still were not getting the intensity and fear that permeated our communities of color. I felt that I needed to do more, not only within Accenture but externally as well. I understood the amount of pain people of color were feeling and I could see the incredible pain that Black people were feeling. I also knew how so many people outside of these communities wanted to help but did not know how.

At that moment, I decided that I was going to step out of my comfort zone, pull from my brand of courage, and write a blog about what we need from our allies. I sat down, said a prayer for guidance, and with a racing heart, I started to write a blog post called *To Be Completely Silent Is Really Loud*. It offered guidance for those who were struggling as to how they could engage with the African American/Black community in this moment of pain, about how allies who may have been feeling awkward could show up for communities of color by creating space for empathy, about how to support people in this moment of need and not stay silent. Little did I know that my words would go on to be shared thousands of times, including by some leaders across industries. I received so many calls, text messages, and emails from people sharing their appreciation. One particular message said, "Nellie, I was trying to figure out how I could have conversations with people about this, should I have a conversation, how would I start, what would I say. Then I read your blog and I got the answers. Thank you."

Once again, tapping into my brand of courage gave me the confidence to put forth a message that needed to be heard in the moment. The murder of George Floyd had a global impact.

No longer could people ignore racism, injustice, and the role we each play in solving for human rights.

Building a More Inclusive Environment One Relationship at a Time

Our differences, biases, and lived experiences all play a role in how we engage with others. It concerns me when leaders say they don't understand the challenges that diverse communities face. It also concerns me when nondiverse leaders push back against people who question the inclusiveness of their company's environment. They see themselves as approachable with an open-door policy, so they don't understand when people voice their difficulties in feeling included within the culture.

Denying someone else's feelings of exclusion, based on your own personal assessment and your perspective of the culture as you are experiencing it, is exactly what prevents people from seeing the change that is required within their organization.

However, denying someone else's feelings of exclusion, based on your own personal assessment and your perspective of the culture as you are experiencing it, is exactly what prevents people from seeing the change that is required within their organizations. Wouldn't it be simple for people to boundlessly thrive if we entered corporate cultures that were immune from negative diversity-related societal influences and bias?

The reality is that building an inclusive environment takes work, and if we pause to see it through the lens of acknowledging the differences and biases that prevent us from having immediate and relatable connections, we would at the very least make informed decisions in that moment. We should ask ourselves, "Am I acknowledging that others may not be experiencing this environment as I am?' An inclusive environment begins with recognizing the gaps—and in some cases, those gaps are glaring. So the next time you are engaging with someone of a different diverse background, ask yourself what you can do to close those gaps and make it an inclusive experience. Better yet, choose to extend yourself and intentionally pull people into your circle who would not traditionally or naturally be there.

Questions for Consideration

1. Where do you believe your organization is in relation to the DE&I Maturity Framework?

2. How are you contributing and engaging in the evolution of an inclusive culture?

3. How is your role as a DE&I practitioner being valued within your organization? How are you supporting DE&I practitioners?

Network Like It's Your Own Dance Floor

Salsa dancing was a significant part of my young adult life. My friends and I had our game plan down to a science, frequenting clubs in New York like the Copacabana (or Copa, as we knew it), La Epoca, Chez Sensual, and many others. From Manhattan to the Bronx, we knew where to find the best salsa music and the best dance partners. We would befriend the deejays to ensure that our song requests were played. Then we'd scope out the dance floors for any talented new dancers and make our way towards them. Just like that, we were on the dance floor showcasing our best moves with the best partners. We were in our flow, our groove, with our best dance skills in full confident display and our energy soaring. Our clubbing attire was right on point, and our self-empowerment in full effect! We looked good and felt good, all while having some of the most carefree and magical moments of our lives. We were savvy and intentional, displaying confidence even when some dance moves challenged us. We wanted to be seen in those salsa clubs, and we figured out exactly how to make it happen.

Reminiscing on those days, I now recognize that we had identified and implemented the necessary steps to effectively reach our goals. We knew where to go and whom to align with. We figured out how to be seen and engaged with the people who could help us evolve our skills. We were unapologetically claiming our space and showing up. Basically, we knew how to effectively build relationships and network. Of course, I didn't know what to call it that back then, but that's exactly what we were doing, and we were really skilled at it. So how did I go from victoriously carving out and confidently owning my space on the dancefloors of New York City to sheepishly retreating to the ladies' room for the entirety of my first corporate networking event?

During my first year with Accenture, I was asked to attend an event at the Marriott Marquis Hotel in Times Square. A lot of leaders would be in attendance, and I was excited about being invited. Walking into the room, I was overwhelmed by the beauty of a massive chandelier hanging from the ceiling. The dark wood walls were so impeccably polished that they reflected the silhouettes of people as they moved around the room. I was in awe. I felt as though I had walked onto a movie set. But those feelings soon turned to panic. I didn't know anyone, and I didn't have any members of my team to lean on. Walking around the room for the first time, I observed the attendees in groups talking and laughing. Not connecting with anyone on my first stroll, I decided to take a couple more walks around the room. But I still couldn't find the confidence to insert myself in any of the conversations. My blood rushed through my ears as the sounds of people's voices grew increasingly louder.

Uncomfortable and unsettled, I decided to go into the ladies restroom to clear my head and bring down my heart rate. I was greeted by an amazing Latina woman who was working in the powder room section. As we effortlessly began talking, I found her relatable, friendly, and welcoming—all the things I couldn't find from the attendees in that massively beautiful reception room. The ease of my conversation with her inspired me to give it another shot, and I went back into the event determined to connect with someone. Instead, I ended up on a line to order a drink. When the bartender asked what he could get me, I responded with a smile, "Water please." It felt like a simple answer to a simple question. Well, even that quickly became unfamiliar to me as the bartender asked in very rapid pace, "Sparkling, still, lemon, or lime?" Huh? Smile gone! Believe it or not, I had never tasted sparkling water before and for sure had never put lemon or lime in my "still" tap water. So out of sheer frustration, I responded, "You choose." Bad choice. My taste buds did not appreciate what felt like an assault of bubbly and bitter lime-tasting sparkling water. I felt such a sense of personal disappointment as I quickly placed that cup down.

I tuned into the voices once again, but it was painfully clear that my own silence was louder in my head than those hundreds of voices together. I spent most of my first networking event in that ladies room. That's where I found my comfort zone. This incredibly relatable woman was doing her job beautifully, but I was doing mine horribly.

I know many in that event noticed me walking around alone several times, but not one thought of pulling me into their conversation. So when people ask me for an example of lack of inclusion within a culture, I say, "Think about a networking event hosted by your organization. Think about how much easier it is to be there and be present when you know the people who are in attendance—your colleagues, team members, and leaders. Now picture yourself in a small group while you are at this networking event. You are engaged and maybe even enjoying yourself. You look up to see someone walking around the room alone, and it is obvious the person has not found a connection. This is your moment of choice. Are you going to act with an inclusive mindset and invite this person into your group, or are you going to ignore this individual and let them keep walking around the room trying to find that connection?"

The truth is that networking is not an effortless process. It takes time, commitment, energy, and planning. In many cases, even after putting in the effort, some people still have a difficult time engaging comfortably. But we must find our own ease with it. That requires a thoughtful contemplation as to why we are not relaxed and confident in these situations. Could it be, for example, that you're not knowledgeable about the topic everyone in the room is discussing? I remember one dinner I attended where I felt completely out of my element and couldn't figure out why. So I stepped away and asked myself, "Why are you feeling this way?" I needed to identify the source. I had become used to being one of a few people of color in the room, and I was able to rule that out as the source of my discomfort. I had also built great relationships with several of my colleagues in attendance, which made my uneasiness even more perplexing. After a bit more internal assessment, I finally got it. It wasn't the composition of the people in the room; it was the topic of discussion that everyone was engaged in—technology and blockchain. I was not able to relate because I was not well informed about that part of the business.

Instead of leaving the dinner, I did what I had heard our current CEO Julie Sweet say so many times: "Be a continuous learner. Don't be afraid to ask or say you don't understand."

Inspired by those words, I selected my target audience within the attendees, strategically picked the opportune time to insert myself, and said, "I want to learn more and need to make time for it. Where do you suggest I start?" Immediately, I felt more at ease as recommendations started pouring in from the group. Sometimes we must acknowledge how we are feeling and step away to assess why we are feeling that way. Don't default to the reactions that feel familiar without considering what other factors may be driving your response.

Relationship Building

It's difficult to predict the overall value of relationships. While some help you in the moment, others may unexpectedly prove beneficial 20 or more years later. So how do we nurture all our networks—both internally and externally—to leverage them for a mutual win? How can we discover ways to authentically engage in seeking, building, and nurturing relationships inclusive of various diverse identities? How do we motivate ourselves to push through and break through barriers?

There are generally three key landing points of the corporate journey: entry level, middle management, and senior executive. Relationships are critical to each of them, with every stage requiring four very important actions:

- Gaining the confidence to network by understanding why it is important, and practicing scenarios
- Making yourself available and choosing to prioritize relationship building even though it may not be something you enjoy doing
- Committing to follow-up by listening and being present in the moment, so you can decide whom you want to follow up with
- Nurturing relationships by understanding why they are critical or valuable to your journey

These actions should fluidly continue throughout each stage of the corporate journey, with an understanding that our focus and needs often shift how we prioritize their importance. What do I mean by that? Focus and need evolve as our careers evolve, exemplified by the distinctive characteristics associated with each stage. Relationships within our career journey are essential, motivating, and rewarding, so we need to prioritize building and fostering them. We all want to feel valued. We want to work with colleagues we trust. We want to feel inspired to deliver at our best, expand our roles, and reach new professional heights. We can achieve each of these aspirations through relationship building. But let's be realistic. There are only so many hours in a day and it's challenging to devote time and energy to everything we have outlined as important. That challenge forces us to make choices that prioritize some things while deprioritizing others, which is fine and fair. As we steer through these decisions, we need to make choices that best position us to reach our goals. Identifying key people to build relationships with is one choice that should be prioritized. The insights that you will receive from this network will stretch your thinking and challenge you to consider new possibilities.

I recently sat down with a junior woman of color for an introductory "get to know you" meeting. In the middle of the conversation, I asked, "So what are your goals? Where do you see yourself careerwise in the next five years or so?"

She responded, "I see myself expanding my current scope, supervising people, and adding value to the group I am currently aligned to."

I looked at her and smiled before responding, "Well, let's dive into that. Your answer does not speak to what level you want to reach. You did not mention extending yourself beyond your current aligned group or considering other areas of the organization that will position you for upskilling and gaining different sets of experiences." I then asked her some questions that I hoped would push her outside of her comfort zone. "Do you really want to be within your current group doing the same thing for the next five years? Are you limiting yourself? What are other areas of the organization that excite you and are aligned to your career interests?"

I could see her face light up as if she had just opened a box to discover a variety of exciting possibilities. She smiled at me and said, "I had not seen myself as someone who would be considered for other areas outside of my current team. But now I am walking away with the understanding that I need to reset and think bigger. How do I even start the process of positioning myself for these opportunities?"

I chose to devote my energy to this young woman because I believed that my contributions and influence would add value to her and to the organization. She made a decision to invest in our relationship. The impact was a success, ultimately leading to a positive outcome.

Sometimes that positivity can be tainted by misplaced expectations. Leaders must be willing to let those to whom they devote their time fly on their own instead of expecting them always to follow their lead, almost as if demanding some sort of loyalty in return. We must give those we guide and coach the space to disengage as they deem appropriate for themselves. While some relationships will be long lasting, others will be short lived, and that is perfectly fine. Often, the mutual benefit of the relationship reaches its purpose and runs its course. But sometimes relationships transcend to long-lasting trusted advisors and even friends. Each scenario is worthy of value as each serves its own productive purpose. And with each professional relationship there is always an opportunity to learn and evolve from having exposure to one another.

Opportunity Squandered

I previously talked we talked about the difficulty of asking for help when personal issues interfere with our professional responsibilities. But what happens when that same source of hesitance keeps us from seizing opportunities for professional growth?

During a recent conversation, a senior colleague talked about how incredibly challenging it is for him to simply make a request from a business contact. He shared how he is always available and finds joy in being known as someone who supports others. But he also deals with feeling depleted by the lack of support he receives in return. He told me that he is constantly frustrated with himself. When I asked him to what he attributed these feelings, he admitted with some discomfort, "I don't know how to comfortably make an ask without feeling needy or incapable of navigating through my role without help. I was raised to handle everything on my own, be of service to others, and never be a nuisance."

I quickly responded, "You know we need to break that ongoing cycle of thinking and you have to commit to starting today."

It was a familiar story for me, as it is for so many people trying to traverse the corporate landscape. But how do we break that cycle? For starters, we must flip the script on the narrative. Instead of thinking, "I don't want to be a bother," or "I don't want to impose," we need to tell ourselves, "This person would

If we are to seek out the essential connections and guidance we deserve, we can't keep rationalizing the limitations we place on ourselves.

welcome me reaching out." Instead of saying, "I don't think my current questions are that important or merit me asking someone for direction or help," we should tell ourselves, "I do not need to measure the substance of my questions, nor do they need to be incredibly impressive ones. I simply need to ask for direction and guidance for what is important for me to address at this moment." We must position ourselves to leverage relationships without the negative way we frame the narrative. If we are to seek out the essential connections and guidance we deserve, we can't keep rationalizing the limitations we place on ourselves. Instead, we must embrace the narrative that when we have invested time in building these relationships, the act of reaching out is part of the natural progression and evolution.

As we build essential connections and seek guidance, we should consider what we hope to accomplish through these opportunities and what seeds we want to plant about ourselves through the stories we share. These are considerations that I wish I would've thought about very junior in my career when I was given the opportunity to have dinner with our CEO at the time. We were visiting a college campus where he was invited to be a keynote speaker, and my role was to support his visit and ensure all went without a single hitch. At the event, I sat proudly listening to my CEO as he addressed the students. Through my lens, I saw a beautiful sea of students of color. I felt a great sense of accomplishment being in a position to experience that moment. It was the mid-'90s, and for the first time in our history, our CEO was spending time at an HBCU. Even more amazing was the fact that I had a whole lot to do with getting him there! I was so excited at the time. But as I reflected later, I realized that my inexperience and lack of awareness caused me to miss a rare and major opportunity to network with the CEO. Why didn't I plan better? Why didn't I reach out in advance and seek advice from trusted advisors regarding this opportunity? What should I have done differently?

What I learned early on from that botched opportunity was that I needed to slow down and realize the importance and significance of these types of professional relationships and opportunities. It would have been incredibly valuable for me to have a mentor advising me on how to engage with our CEO. One thing became crystal clear to me—I needed to build trusted advisor relationships. There, as if perfectly timed by the universe, entered Andrew Jackson!

At that time, Andrew was the second-highest-ranking African American leader at Accenture. I had heard he was also leading efforts to attract people of color to the organization. Given that I was doing the same thing, I reached out to introduce myself. It was perfect timing as I was working towards bringing African American and Hispanic executives together. Within that introduction, I shared why it was important for him to know me. I mean, talk about being on a mission—classic! And just like that we became a force, united in paving the way to cast a wider net and build a strong and sustainable diversity program. There was no need to spend time on all the cautionary steps. There were no questions about getting each other's vision or doubts about being vulnerable with each other. Our lived experiences as two people of color navigating the challenges of corporate culture quickly enabled us to gel and partner. From the start, we told each other how it was, with no holds barred and no checking filters. We courageously broke down barriers because we understood each other and immediately valued the "power of two." We were on a mission, united by the genuine belief that our organization was a place where we wanted others like us to have an opportunity to join and succeed. We just needed to open and widen that path.

When you can engage and partner with colleagues who are relatable, who share experiences and cultural nuances, it is undeniably empowering. Andrew and I didn't have to worry about biases; we had none towards each other because we understood the strength of what we both brought to our respective roles. We also didn't have dramatic cultural differences that could've been misunderstood or perceived as a flaw to our leadership or skills. That is the power of representation and why it is so critically important across all aspects of diversity. You are productive from the start, because from the start, there is that sense of commonality and belonging.

Andrew and I built a network of incredible people of color. We didn't wait for permission or an anointing to lead in solving for closing the gaps. We reached out to other leaders that represented our ethnicities. We rallied colleagues and leaders to join our efforts. Then we reached out to the influential leaders who could align the funding we needed to activate our vision. The result was an increased outreach of recruiting sources, membership within diverse external organizations. We activated members of our network to become mentors and be faculty in leadership development programs. Through that process we also crafted an incredible friendship, originating through our professional lives but transcending to our personal families, as well as an extended family of all those we coached, sponsored, and lifted.

Help Me Understand

As most typically do when the plane lands, I quickly switched off my phone's airplane mode and started catching up on all I had missed during my flight. As I was going through my messages, I saw one from a colleague I had mentored for years. He was sharing a decision he made about stepping down from his plus-one role, which is an activity that goes above and beyond an employee's regular job duties or responsibilities. Employees sometimes choose to take on these voluntary roles to further contribute to the organization's goals while also evolving their own skills, raising visibility, and expanding their professional network. This colleague didn't feel he had the bandwidth to handle the extra tasks. My network of mentees, team members, and colleagues know that when they hear me question, "What were you thinking?" or hear me say, "Help me understand," that typically means that we are about to dive into a deep conversation. So when we jumped on a call, my first words were a combination of the two. "What were you thinking? Please help me understand because I don't agree." I started down the airport escalator as he began sharing his rationale. I became so invested in our conversation that I failed to realize that I was continuously going down the wrong set of escalators. I must have looked so disheveled to anyone who noticed in that moment. Just as he finished laying out the thought process that led to his decision, I finally realized that I had been going up and down the same escalator. Despite my frantic airport circling, I thanked him in a nurturing way for sharing his rationale with me.

I quickly deciphered that this decision was motivated by urgency rather than strategic thinking. So, true to form, I went in with questions. Are you aware that by stepping away from this role, you are giving up access to the C-suite? Do you recognize that through this role you have been provided incredible exposure among influential leaders? Have you paused to assess how your brand has evolved since taking on the role? Is this exposure still important to you and your career goals? What other options may there be to meet your desire to reduce your workload? I think of these as the five lead-ins:

- Are you aware. . .
- Do you recognize. . .
- Have you paused. . .
- Is this still important. . .
- What other options. . .

They can prove extremely powerful in contemplative situations where individuals need to carefully think through their decisions. But helping people through these lead-ins can be challenging when relationships have not been established. As leaders, we sometimes recognize the need for important and key conversations with individuals, whether they are in junior positions to ourselves or in positions as our peers and colleagues. But we may feel a sense of confinement as we search for the courage to reach out, particularly when there is not an already established relationship. We may feel like we have not earned the privilege or permission to dive deep into these conversations, so we measure our words for fear of causing discomfort for either party. This can lead to missed opportunities to have the necessary conversations that are required to make better strategic and informed decisions, which underscores the importance of mentor-mentee relationships. This is why it is essential that we also create a network of those who share our experiences and can break through the perceived confinements placed on us by others to simply have authentic conversations.

I walked him through various other options, helping him recognize what he would be giving up. He was able to be vulnerable in a safe space, and our conversation resulted in a well-thought-out decision to reach a better outcome. That's the power of trusted and relatable relationships.

The Power of Elevating External Organizational Relationships

Building professional relationships is not limited to the people within your organization. However, our respective organizations don't always naturally create that space. Sometimes we can feel unseen and lost in the magnitude of our corporate culture, almost as if we are relegated to a corner where opportunities for meaningful exposure are limited.

We have all experienced moments in our lives where we felt comfortable, relaxed, and welcomed. It's a beautiful feeling, and chances are that you were around people who knew you well, who embraced and accepted you. They are the people who provide you with an instant feeling of belonging with mutual cultural connections, relatable subtle gestures, identities, and warm greetings. That's the potential impact of building relationships within external organizations that serve diverse communities.

In most cases, these not-for-profit organizations provide a sense of immediate belonging and familiarity. They offer an environment where you can be yourself without needing to code-switch and shield yourself from depleting, hurtful, and damaging biases. These organizations serve multiple purposes to provide a focused approach, while solving to close gaps, advocating for communities, and in some cases influencing government policies.

When contemplating membership with an external organization, there are some important considerations:

- Identify an organization whose mission is important to you.
- What part of the organization do you want to engage in? Does it provide opportunities to address issues you care about and solve for major gaps?
- How do you get involved in some of their key high-profile events?

Don't just join to join. Make an investment in you. Have a plan to be an active participant, potentially joining their committees, advisory councils, or board to benefit from the networking.

I have always sought out external organizations with a focus for the Accenture brand. But I evolved the way I value some of these organizations as I recognized that they also played a significant role in expanding their members' external footprints and networks. Just like my association with ALPFA, two additional examples have been my engagement with the Hispanic Technology Executive Council (HITEC), a network of Hispanic tech leaders, and Latina Style, Inc., an organization committed to highlighting and recognizing professional Latinas in corporate America. Not only do our partnerships add value for Accenture, but every honor and award that I receive also showcases my brand. External organizations help us to be seen, lifting our brand and connecting us to wider networks. They validate our journey and positioning while influencing our organizations to celebrate us. That is the power of these external organizations.

Questions for Consideration

1. What priority are you placing on networking?

2. How is your external presence and engagement increasing your visibility and solving for your community?

3. How are you pausing to reflect on the current stage of your professional journey and how are you encouraging others to do the same?

I Am Where I Earned to Be

Today, more than 35 years into my Accenture journey, I am aware of what it takes to claim my earned space and have my voice heard. I have learned how to position myself to be seen and have my value acknowledged. I have assertively positioned myself, and I have recognized how each career decision impacted my overall wealth-generating goal. Claiming my earned space has required honest conversations with myself about what is impacting me, while challenging myself to move out of the comfort zones that could have limited my opportunities and kept me stagnant. I have learned how to differentiate between emotionally charged decisions versus those that are well thought out. I have surrounded myself with motivators, and have assertively communicated my career goals with leaders, holding them accountable as my advocates. To claim my earned space, I have sought to learn and evolve, but I have also given myself grace when my mistakes led to tough or disheartening lessons. I have used the lessons to teach and bring others along on my journey while also helping them navigate their own paths. It has been a truly incredible ride with many incredible people, and it was only possible because I refused to let biases define me, and unapologetically defined my brand of courage.

Yet even with all the amazing things that I have experienced, accomplished, and learned, I still find myself triggered when someone doubts or dismisses my abilities. It's a familiar scenario for many people of color in high-ranking leadership positions, usually starting with a question like "How did *you* get here?" I do realize that this may sound like a harmless inquiry on the surface, but when you are aware of the microinequities and ongoing biases that people have, you recognize the underlying insinuations: that I am unqualified, or that somebody handed me my role instead of me earning it. It is an infuriating position to be in, and a constant reminder that asserting your worth is an ongoing requirement for some of us. Unfortunately, these types of questions never go away, no matter how senior you are in your journey.

During a recent conversation with a colleague whom I highly respect and admire, he asked, "So, tell me, how did you end up with this gig you now have. How did you work *that one* out?" I was immediately triggered. It was not just the sentiment associated with this question, but his use of the term "gig" felt demeaning. It felt even worse because it came from a person whom I helped in courageous and relentless ways. I was completely taken aback by the question, but even in my discomfort I chose not to feed into this narrative. I was certainly at the point in my career journey where justifying any of my accomplishments was no longer something I wanted to devote my energy to, and I was annoyed that he expected me to do so.

I took a deep breath, leaned back on my chair, and made direct eye contact with him. Then I very calmly and intentionally said, "I am where I have earned to be." Mic drop!

I could see him taking in my response as he dropped his head for a moment. When he finally looked up at me, he sheepishly responded, "And where we all need you to be!"

Own It!

Very early on in my career, I constantly heard leaders say, "Own your career." I immediately felt the intensity of that statement as a reinforcement to make your own decisions, stand by your choices, and own the outcomes. While I was initially unsure how to incorporate that powerful message into my journey, I knew that dismissing such valuable advice would not be wise. I needed to immediately integrate this formidable mantra into how I managed my experiences, and that is exactly what I did. Since then, I have probably used the term thousands of times in my coaching sessions. For the most part, people quickly embrace it. But a recent conversation required me to stop and truly break it down.

I had connected with a woman who aspired to reach leadership levels. When I spoke to her about the importance of owning her career, she frantically responded, "What does that really mean? How do I own my career? What do I need to do? It sounds hard. I need details. I need clear steps!" She was very animated at first, and I felt her exasperation. But once she gathered her thoughts, she said, "You are suggesting I become more visible with influential leaders, but I don't feel now is the best time given everyone's stressors. How would it be perceived in the climate we are experiencing?"

I quickly laid out three thought-provoking responses:

- Assess your current state. Pause to be honest with yourself about how you are truly experiencing your career path.
  - How do feel about where you are in your professional journey?
  - What would it look like to dream bigger and what would that require?

No matter how junior or senior we are in our profession, being eagerly curious about the next opportunity provides an advantage.

- What path seems realistic and necessary to you as you think about achieving your goals?
  - Identify your blockers. Consider the limitations that you are placing within your own path.
  - Are you talking yourself out of stretch roles? How many have you already passed on and how does that make you feel?
  - Are you making excuses for not engaging with influential leaders?
  - What personal narrative is limiting your professional advancement?
- Take action. Recognize the steps that are essential for taking ownership of your career.
  - What are the short- and long-term steps you should take to assertively pursue greater career heights?
  - Have you crafted a career aspiration pitch that positions you to share your goals and aspirations in front of leaders?
  - Do you have a plan of action to increase your exposure and take advantage of visible opportunities?

Owning your career requires you to position yourself assertively, intentionally, and strategically. However, you cannot effectively do so without allocating time to gauge where you are, analyzing your progress towards your goals and establishing your preparedness for the ventures that lie ahead. It requires you to have a personal agreement with yourself that real self-talk is essential and challenging yourself is a must.

During a career fair several years ago, I was walking towards our Accenture booth when I saw a big sign that read, "The Accenture Adventure." Reading it gave me an immediate jolt of energy and I quickly turned towards a group of college students who were waiting to speak with some of our representatives. I pointed to the sign and declared, "My Accenture Adventure has taken me from the Bronx to Africa, Argentina, Australia, Brazil, Canada, China, France, Germany, India, Ireland, Italy, Japan, Malaysia, Mexico, the Netherlands, Singapore, South Korea, Spain, and the United Kingdom. It truly has been an adventure!" I paused to let my words sink in for a minute, and then followed by saying, "And to think. . .when I was about your age, my biggest travel dream was going to Florida someday." While we all got a good laugh from that, the weight of it was not lost on me.

For me, the Accenture Adventure represents the choice to take risks and experience the world, a boldness that was encouraged within me through the sponsorship of some amazing leaders. When I entered this incredible organization, I had no expectation of traveling the world. Global travel was not supposed to be part of the script for someone like me. That was my personal belief. But fortunately for me, throughout my junior and mid-level career, several leaders believed differently and propelled me in that direction.

As I gained more experience and insight, I also positioned myself to think differently. Instead of shutting myself out of new opportunities, I would think, "Why not give myself that chance?" Now, in all honesty, it was an ongoing choice. There were numerous times when I embraced new opportunities and then regretted my decisions due to fear. I would sometimes catch myself thinking, "Why in the heck did you volunteer to take that on? Do you really want to fly half way across the world?" Reflecting on those thoughts now, I recognize that my conditioned thinking and limited belief had just not fully evolved to catch up with what I was destined to do. I now know that my desire to step out of my comfort zone, evolve, and take risks was always fully and excitedly present within me.

I used to hear various leaders favor those team members who took on short-term or long-term international assignments. These expat opportunities required physically moving and making a commitment to live in other countries for at least a year. Individuals who chose these paths were immediately credentialed to an elevated level, and I remember hearing comments about them like, "You know she is so well-versed in other cultures because she spent time working in China and India," or "He is great. He did three international assignments, one of which was in France."

These characterizations captured my curiosity through various lenses. I thought it was quite brave for someone to pick up, step away from familiarity, and embark onto the unknown in other countries. But I also thought about the disadvantage that existed for those who did not have the luxury to pursue expat assignments due to personal limitations. And as a result, they were not given the favorable edge. I did not want that to be my reality, and I had to figure out a way to work around that partiality. So, despite my fears and what I believed to be my lack of interest in traveling outside of the United States, I positioned myself to expand my scope. I was intensely driven by the goal of solving for inclusion and diversity throughout the world. I intentionally chose to knock down the barriers and creatively solve to expand my global experience. I might not have been able to pick up and move to another country, but I could certainly make a significant impact across multiple countries by working on-site for days or weeks at a time through shorter but highly impactful trips.

Traveling so much for work was not easy. I found myself at odds with my ambitions and the cultural responsibilities that had been engrained in me that dictated I put my family first above all, even my ambition. Questions lingered heavily on me. How am I going to make this work? How do I silence my own fears? What sacrifices am I willing to make, and at what expense? How will this impact my family? Am I being selfish for wanting this experience? There was a lot of guilt placed on me by others, as well as myself, but I discovered one very important thing. I didn't need to have all the answers in order to pursue my goals. Through each experience, I could adjust and readjust. Some of the adjustments came after tears, others through smiles. Some lessons were tough, while others were fun and enjoyable. But through it all, I learned the value in gifting myself the courage to clear hurdles and the permission not to always get it right.

Now What?

One pesky question has consistently lingered throughout every stage of my career journey, and it has annoyingly intensified with each new stage. "Now what?" While these two words have often been the source of significant unease, they have also kept me motivated by making me think about my career with a wide and holistic lens.

No matter how junior or senior we are in our profession, being eagerly curious about the next opportunity provides an advantage. Whether we are at the start of our journey, somewhere in the middle, or reaching the end of a long and successful career, the "Now what?" question holds us accountable to continuously examine our professional choices and how we feel about them. This personal career analysis should also include an appraisal of our financial health and where we are with evolving our compensation and wealth goals. Are we at a point in our journey where a lot of runway remains for our maximum earning potential or are we facing a runway that's shorter? Are we on track to meet our goals around building assets and creating generational wealth? With an honest assessment of our current financial situation, as well as our personal and professional goals, we should have a better understanding of where we desire to go.

Throughout your journey, ask yourself these reflective and sometimes challenging questions:

Entry level: It's time to be all things curious.

- How does my organization generate revenue?
- Who are the key leaders?
- Where are my current and future influencers who will support me in achieving my career aspirations?
- What are the hot skills I should be pursuing?
- Do I feel confident as a representative of my diverse background, energized and prepared to position myself to be Seen, Heard, and Valued?
- Am I feeling confident? If not, why not?
- What am I doing to support my emotional well-being?

Middle management: It's time to evaluate.

- Am I aligned with my passion, either directly through my role or indirectly through the power of my role?
- Have I met my aspirational career goals thus far?
- Is this the environment where I want to continue aligning my skills, time, and energy? Is it time to consider a shift in my career path?
- Am I committed to aggressively doing what it takes to accelerate my career?

- As a representative of my diversity, do I feel that I have been Seen, Heard, and Valued?
- Am I feeling confident? If not, why not?
- What am I doing to support my emotional well-being?

Senior executive: It's time to reflect and plan.

- Who is represented in my succession plan?
- How am I lifting others within my organization?
- Am I leveraging my leadership level, resources, and organizational brand to solve for community gaps?
- Have I taken the time to start planning my next phase?
- What role am I playing in making others feel Seen, Heard, and Valued?
- Am I feeling confident? If not, why not?
- What am I doing to support my emotional well-being?

You will notice that Seen, Heard, and Valued is consistent through each of these stages. Being *Seen* can show up in many ways within an organization. It means you and your contributions are being recognized, accepted, and respected. You have been well positioned for visibility to others within the organization. Feeling *Heard* is critically important to our careers. You have a platform by which to effectively contribute. Your voice is listened to through your sharing of insights and expertise. You are sought after by peers, colleagues, and leaders. You experience *Value* when there is a sense of achievement and importance, where your contributions are embraced, and the organization is investing in your continued development and growth. When "Seen, Heard, and Valued" are aligned and part of an individual's experience, it creates a full sense of Belonging!

There are many reasons why we may fail to have these important conversations with ourselves. Perhaps we have settled into the comfort of our current accomplishments. After all, many of us have already reached heights far beyond what we ever considered possible. It may feel selfish or greedy to believe that we deserve more or to assertively plan our "next." We may have also decided that greater financial aspirations are unattainable, convincing ourselves that our earning potential is maxed out. But these self-limiting narratives keep us from achieving our financial goals. They stop us from even considering the wealth opportunities in front of us and prevent us from aiming for professional roles with highly lucrative compensation packages. If reaching a certain wealth model is important, we must position ourselves to get there. We should be prepared to take advantage by intentionally claiming opportunities to negotiate and advocate for ourselves so that no money is left on the table.

It is equally important to note that everyone's journey varies. Some of us have no desire for a higher-paying position. We may be planning a step back from our fast-paced careers. We may have a short-term situation that requires our attention at home, or we may seek to develop a better integration of our personal and professional lives overall. Whatever our ultimate goal is, we still need to consider how our plans will ultimately impact our desired wealth model and, conversely, how our wealth model affects our short- and long-term plans.

Compete Is Not a Dirty Word

I was at a formal awards luncheon receiving an award. As I typically do, I worked the room saying hello to the people I knew, meeting new acquaintances and congratulating my fellow awardees.

Upon sitting at my assigned table, I noticed Sol Trujillo, a very reputable Latino executive, approach one of my fellow awardees to congratulate her. I had initially learned of him years before, when I was invited to participate in a conference call where he was the featured speaker. At the time, he was the CEO of one of our highly regarded clients. I was immediately impressed and positively impacted by his presentation, especially because it was my first time experiencing a Hispanic American at this level.

Now, years later, this esteemed leader was right in front of me, and while I so desperately wanted to engage in his conversation with my fellow award recipient, it was clear that interrupting them was not the right move. After they parted ways, I stared at him as he walked away. Yes, this was an opportunity missed at the time, but I told myself that it would not be missed again. I told myself that the day would come when he would know who I am. I knew my network would keep expanding, and collaborating with him could yield incredible results, because he was very business driven and part of a very senior circle. So I was determined to bring my affirmation to life.

A few years later, the opportunity to engage with him presented itself again. Now retired from his most recent CEO post, he has impressively co-founded L'ATTITUDE. Today, Sol and I call each other friends. We have had thought-provoking conversations, collaborating to solve for closing gaps within our community. We have ideated and actioned things that are of equal importance to both us and our community at large, while bringing others along as well.

I recall an event where I had the honor of interviewing Sol. I asked him, "Beyond being seen, heard, and valued, what else do we need to do as a community?"

In a very assertive and concerned manner, he answered, "We need to compete. We shy away from competing and we must change that."

His response was so impactful for me. He was so sure about his assertion, and it made me question my own level of competitiveness. I knew I had been competing assertively throughout my journey, but I just had not called it competing. Sol made me realize that I needed to share this aspect of my career and encourage other people to compete without fear. So, shortly after that interview, I began doing just that.

Just as we altered our perception of the word "aggressive" to "assertive" when describing women, we need to stop perceiving "compete" as a dirty word. It is a word we need to incorporate and embrace. Especially among many people of color, the prospect of competing within a corporate environment feels uncomfortable, particularly because many of us have never been taught the necessary skills. Instead, we often grew up with conversations about working better and harder simply to be considered equal, but we need to remind ourselves that we are intellectually and professionally at the level of our peers. When competing was encouraged, it was rarely in relation to a corporate environment.

The definition of competing speaks about outdoing someone and striving to gain something through the defeat of others. However, for many people of color, outdoing a colleague could mean attracting negative attention, biases, and envy. We worry about being seen as a threat by others who don't look like us and becoming the target of their backlash. But we need to stop looking at competition through the definition by which we have been taught to experience it. Instead, we need to look at it from the perspective of competing to solve for our goals and building our future wealth model. We must get comfortable with competing.

I remember walking away from my interview of Sol thinking, "We are warriors." Each one of us, through our own personal journey, has paved unchartered paths. My opportunity to collaborate with him did not simply happen by wishing it into reality. It came to fruition through my continued focus on positioning myself to be in the right place, with the right skills and power to take advantage of the opportunity. During the process of preparing ourselves for those opportunities we must be our own warriors. We must challenge ourselves to remove barriers, align with influential leaders, identify the value, and take a stance about how we want to position ourselves.

I have a family member who asks the same question every time we engage in conversations about people of color within the corporate sector. "Why do you think we reach a certain level and then totally plateau? There are only a handful who make it to the very top. Why is that?" He then follows that with a long list of accomplished people of color who have seemingly plateaued, although they are still impressive leaders. Each time he asks me that, I can see the angst on his face as he tries to identify what keeps so many people of color from reaching the top senior executive levels. I can tell he wants to understand so that he can overcome the challenges that have plagued those on his list.

I find myself wanting to give him one clear-cut answer, but there really isn't just one. There are so many factors at work, including cultural environment and a lack of sponsorship. During one of our more recent conversations, competing came to mind. I realized that, if I considered the factors that I have witnessed propel people of color, women, and diverse individuals overall, assertively competing is high on the list. It's part of a formula that also includes constant upskilling, strategic networking, inclusive environments, and committed sponsors. All these things are required to move us beyond the plateau status. Though many are still working on one or more of these factors, we must stay willing and inspired to tap into our warrior side. Make commitments to yourself to stand out and continuously position yourself for growth.

Are You Really Empowered?

My experiences throughout my corporate journey have ranged from tremendously challenging to incredibly rewarding. I have fought countless battles with passionate intensity, winning some and losing others. Some battles scared me, some intimidated me, some inspired me, and some propelled me to heights of courage I could have never foreseen or predicted. I have privately had my happy dance moments while celebrating key wins. And with similar energy, I have contemplated the losses by diving deep into my understanding of the lessons learned. I have realized that all fights do not warrant full-on battles. I have learned to be thoughtful and informed, to choose wisely and understand the power of timing. I have also grown to value the power of alliances and the team efforts that have led me to partnering with incredible Accenture leaders, colleagues, and peers who harmoniously marched along the same path towards evolving our culture with an unwavering vision of achieving our mission towards equity across communities. Today more than ever, we must display our ongoing commitment to solving for equity and equality.

With every challenge and lesson, I learned more about myself and my empowerment. I recognize that it is not something that just happens without intentionality, and I have developed clarity that I perform at my best when the following is constant.

I confidently:

- Agitate and disrupt with good intentions
- Advocate for myself and others
- Leverage and action my power

I continue to:

- Be my own hype person
- Assertively position myself
- Reject the limitations of my comfort zone

I choose to:

- Be purposeful in starting my day in prayer and ending it in gratitude
- Give myself and others grace
- Unapologetically honor my culture

I commit to:

- Be intentional with the narrative I am feeding myself
- Be mindful of the impact that others have on me
- Set and respect my own boundaries

I condition myself to:

- Be astute at deciphering intentional bias versus uninformed ignorance
- Be conscious of how others may interpret my body language and nonverbal cues

- Intentionally pause to limit emotionally charged reactions and thoughtfully shape my responses

This all may sound daunting, but it doesn't have to be. You can reach your own empowerment by owning and adjusting what you can control. If you show up every day with this mindset, think of the potential and power you will infuse within yourself. Think about the lives you can change and the future that you can craft for yourself and your family.

I also recognize that my time at Accenture has been infused with an incredible opportunity to help, lift, and provide opportunities for people. It is a gift that I graciously receive, which is why I pray purpose into my life every day. Often, people tell me that I changed their lives in some way, which is such a rewarding statement to hear. So when they follow up with asking how they can thank me, my response is easy. Commit to lifting others.

For my 30th work anniversary at Accenture, Ellyn Shook hosted a dinner to celebrate me. Accenture HR leaders from all over the world were in town for a separate event and not only did she include them in the celebration, but she also included my family! It was an exquisite restaurant with amazing colleagues, wonderful gifts, and beautiful flowers. But one of the most precious, unforgettable and always-in-my-heart moments was seeing my mother, who had never before attended any of my work events. When I saw her elegance radiating across the room, I knew this event was about my mother and my family, who sacrificed so much to help me reach the heights of this moment. As each of my colleagues stood up to celebrate me and talk about the impact I have had on so many around the world, all I kept thinking about was how amazing it was to share this moment with my family.

Some of my colleagues teared up as they told their stories, though I resisted letting my emotions engage. But when my daughter stood up, I was blown away by her speech. One particular line truly impacted me. She said, "I used to get upset when my mom would travel as I was younger. As I have gotten older and have seen her impact on so many, I know now that she was meant to be shared with others." The smile on my son's face as he proudly looked back and forth between his sister and me, along with my daughter's beautiful comments, will forever be etched in my heart. What an incredible moment. My husband leaned over at one point and whispered, "You make us so proud; you are special not only to us, but to all you touch."

Throughout my journey, I have chosen to learn, and I have chosen to advocate. I will continuously and courageously claim my earned space, and with an unwavering commitment, I will always reject biases, ignite change, and celebrate the beauty of inclusion!

Acknowledgments

I t is with a heart full of gratitude that I give praise and thank God for the countless blessings that have been bestowed upon me.

There is a saying that your spirit will not let you rest until you have accomplished what you are meant to achieve. This book is one of those things. It had been brewing within me for many years. Then, just over two years ago, I had a conversation with Ellyn Shook, Chief Leadership and Human Resources Officer at Accenture. We talked about my career and my future ambitions. Once I mentioned my writing goals, she excitedly encouraged me to start this book with the full sponsorship and support of Accenture. Sometimes you simply need a person to create the space for you to reach what would otherwise seem like an unattainable goal. Ellyn was this person for me, and for that I wholeheartedly thank her.

I have always believed that people enter your journey at just the right time, exactly when you need them. Throughout this book process, there were several key people who undoubtedly made this book journey possible:

Erika Winston: From the moment I read her work, I wanted her to be a part of my journey. Her creativity, relentless commitment to excellence, and compassion ignited my already courageous and authentic voice throughout this book. Erika was beyond pivotal to the completion of this book. Our partnership evolved into a friendship, and the bond we formed will forever have a special place in my heart.

Carolina Z. Cardoso: There is a question that often comes up as part of the Corporate Pulse Cultural Survey: Do you have a best friend at work? Thankfully, my answer is a resounding *yes*! In our 20-plus-year journey, traveling the world and solving for inclusion, we have positively impacted so many lives together. What I didn't expect was Carolina's unending availability to support me throughout this book writing process. Whether it was to check my thinking, help me move beyond a writer's block moment, or complete some factual checking, she enthusiastically showed up for me each time. Carolina's emotional support was invaluable, and she is incredibly special to me.

Rachea Amdemariam: When I looked up the definition of *guide* it stated, "a person who advises or shows the way to others." Rachea was my incredible guide throughout the writing process. Her nurturing and assertive style provided me with a view and timeline that was necessary to reaching this goal. She managed the project planning, rallying others to come along on the journey to help me achieve this goal. What a gift Rachea has been to me.

Carolyn Monaco: Not only did Carolyn share her expertise in the publishing industry, but she also chose to see the process of this book from a different lens, quickly recognizing its purpose and acknowledging the need for it. Her immediate understanding of the importance of ensuring diversity was key to this journey will forever be appreciated.

Susan Mino: Sometimes people are not aware of how their enthusiasm plays a role in feeding you the energy you need to get started towards a goal. She has been a springboard to keeping me organized, ensuring calendars were in sync and crucial conversations continued to take place. Susan's commitment has been incredibly special.

Throughout the writing process my family has been my pillar of strength. There were moments filled with excitement and others filled with doubt. My mom, husband, daughter, and son each played a unique role in cheering me through the times when the process felt a bit heavy. Although my dad is no longer here physically with me, his presence was spiritually felt and he has been a source of inspiration. Their love continues to lift me!

To every single person whom I have met throughout my 35-plus years with Accenture, each internal and external encounter has played a role in helping me achieve everything that I have accomplished. I want to thank all who have trusted me and allowed me to advocate for them, and all who have taught me lessons, whether they were inspiring or challenging. Thank you for playing an important role in shaping my career.

My hope is that *everyone* will show up each day with empathy and choose to relentlessly advocate for inclusion!

About the Author

For more than three decades, Nellie Borrero has been a voice for change and an unwavering leader committed to the advancement of inclusion, diversity, equity, and equality.

Through her bold actions and relentless advocacy, Nellie has impacted over 500,000 people globally, fostering an environment that rejects bias and ignites change. She is driven by the belief that through leadership accountability and the principle that it's everyone's responsibility to educate, communicate, and raise the awareness of others' unique experiences, people can choose to embrace the beauty of inclusion and celebrate each other's authentic identities. When Nellie joined Accenture in 1986, she quickly recognized an opportunity to evolve the existing corporate culture. This led to the creation of Accenture's first diversity role, where her unyielding perseverance influenced leaders and colleagues to recognize the business advantages of diversity—understanding the power and greater innovation generated by diverse teams.

Nellie has worked across industries and cultures with C-suite professionals to lead Diversity, Equity, and Inclusion (DEI) through sustainable strategies infused with data-driven approaches that accelerate the goal of closing gaps and leading through inclusion. She has developed award-winning programs and earned the company multiple top rankings and recognitions. Her footprint spans around the world, including Australia, Brazil, India, Japan, Spain, South Africa, the UK, and elsewhere.

Nellie is widely recognized for her leadership. Among her many accolades, she has been named to:

- Hispanic Technology Executive Council's Estrella Award (2023)
- Association of Latino Professionals for America's Inaugural Hall of Fame, "Most Powerful Latina" (2022)
- Hispanic Technology Executive Council's Hall of Fame (2022)
- *Latina Style*'s Highest-Ranking Latina (2021)
- *ALPFA*'s "50 Most Powerful Latinas," featured in *Fortune* (2017, 2018)
- *Black Enterprise*'s Top Executives in Corporate Diversity (2016)

Media coverage includes *Forbes*, the *Chicago Tribune*, *Management Consulting* magazine, *Fair360*, *Latina Style* magazine, and National Public Radio (NPR). A sought-after speaker, Nellie is known for her inspirational impact and genuine care for people. She has taken the stage at a wide range of events, such as the Colloquium on Global Diversity, People En Espanol, the Global Summit of Women, SHRM, *Latina Style* Top 50, and Asian Business Roundtable Conference. Nellie has also authored several publications highlighting her expertise.

Nellie earned her BA from Lehman College. She has served on a number of nonprofit boards to be the source for change for today and future generations. Nellie's greatest joy is spending time with her husband, two children, grandson, and extended family.

Journey Line Exercise

The description of how to do a journey line should be included before the journey lines.

At Accenture, we have incorporate the Journey Line exercise into some of our leadership development courses.

A Journey Line is a tool to help you define what moments and events in your past shape and guide your future. This helps to reveal the lessons you have learned in your career and helps you uncover your teachable point of view and the longer term impact of your career and personal decisions. The journey line is a building block of a teachable point of views that can be shared with others. You can focus on just work related points or choose to integrate personal key journey points as well.

How do you create your own Journey Line?

- To begin, plot the emotional ups and downs of your professional development journey
  - Times you felt good about your work
  - Skills and experiences you developed or needed
  - Times you were down about yourself or stressed out
  - Times you were bored
- Label the critical events and the emotional peaks and valleys.
- For each critical event plotted, recall the experiences that led to those moments.

My Journey: The Story Behind What Others See

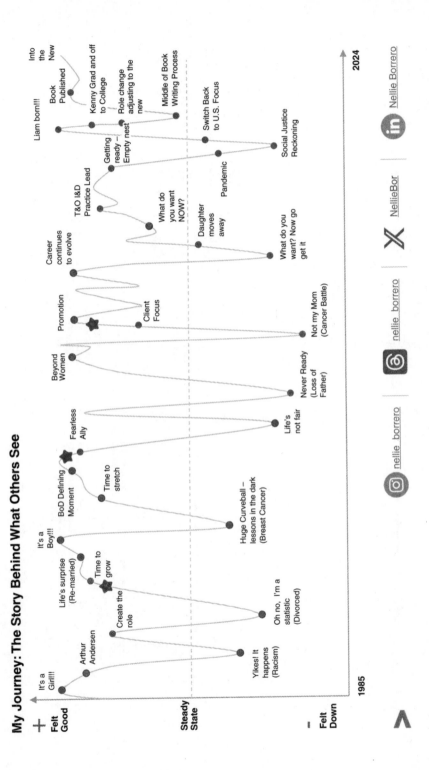

Our history reflects our commitment

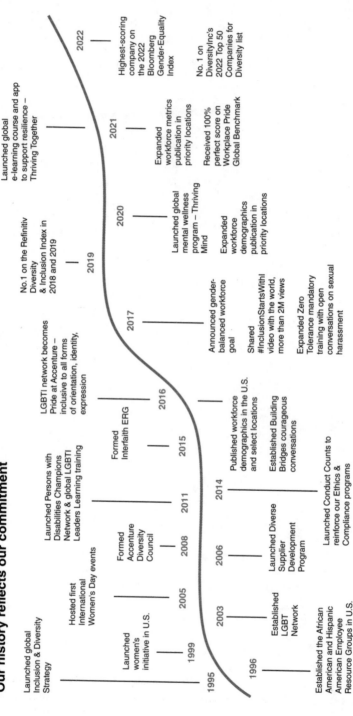

1995 — Launched global Inclusion & Diversity Strategy

1999 — Launched women's initiative in U.S.

2005 — Hosted first International Women's Day events

2008 — Formed Accenture Diversity Council

2011 — Launched Persons with Disabilities Champions Network & global LGBTI Leaders Learning training

2015 — Formed Interfaith ERG

2016 — LGBTI network becomes Pride at Accenture – inclusive to all forms of orientation, identity, expression

2019 — No.1 on the Refinitiv Diversity & Inclusion Index in 2018 and 2019

2021 — Launched global e-learning course and app to support resilience – Thriving Together

1996 — Established the African American and Hispanic American Employee Resource Groups in U.S.

2003 — Established LGBT Network

2006 — Launched Diverse Supplier Development Program

2014 — Launched Conduct Counts to reinforce our Ethics & Compliance programs; Published workforce demographics in the U.S. and select locations; Established Building Bridges courageous conversations

2017 — Announced gender-balanced workforce goal; Shared #InclusionStartsWithI video with the world, more than 2M views; Expanded Zero Tolerance mandatory training with open conversations on sexual harassment

2020 — Launched global mental wellness program – Thriving Mind; Expanded workforce demographics publication in priority locations

2022 — Highest-scoring company on the 2022 Bloomberg Gender-Equality Index

Expanded workforce metrics publication in priority locations; Received 100% perfect score on Workplace Pride Global Benchmark

No. 1 on DiversityInc's 2022 Top 50 Companies for Diversity list

*This is a sample of key actions from our detailed historical timeline.

Index